AFRICANUS HORTON
1835–1883

CHRISTOPHER FYFE is Reader in African History at the University of Edinburgh. A former Government Archivist in Sierra Leone, he is the author of *A History of Sierra Leone* and *Sierra Leone Inheritance,* and editor of E. W. Blyden's *Christianity, Islam and The Negro Race.*

FYFE, Christopher. Africanus Horton, 1835–1883; West African scientist and patriot. Oxford, 1972. 169p map bibl 71-170259. 6.75, 1.95 pa. ISBN 0-19-501501-0
Written by the author of the reasonably well-regarded *A history of Sierra Leone* (CHOICE, Mar. 1965), this book is important because it is the first full-length biography of a West African who more than 100 years ago encouraged his fellow West Africans to develop self-government and who, in the words of David Kimble, "was the first West African who felt it necessary to challenge, seriously and publicly, the widespread belief in the natural inferiority of Africans." Some knowledge of this man and his work should enlighten those who still believe that all Africans before 1870 were barbarians and witch doctors. James Africanus Beale Horton, born of Ibo parents in 1835, received a medical education in Britain, returned to West Africa and served for 20 years as a medical officer in the British Army. He took some part in politics, encouraged the abortive Fanti Confederation, wrote *West African countries and peoples* (CHOICE, May 1970) and worked for the economic development of the area. Based largely on primary materials, this volume, which reads well, is recommended for all libraries with serious

Continued

FYFE

African collections. Less affluent libraries should first acquire David Kimble, *A political history of Ghana* (1963). One map. Index. Undistinguished format.

AFRICANUS HORTON

1835-1883

WEST AFRICAN SCIENTIST

AND PATRIOT

CHRISTOPHER FYFE

Centre of African Studies
University of Edinburgh

NEW YORK
OXFORD UNIVERSITY PRESS
1972

THIS STUDY IS ONE IN A SERIES OF SHORT BIOGRAPHIES OF DISTIN-
GUISHED BLACK AMERICANS AND BLACK AFRICANS, PREPARED UNDER
THE EDITORSHIP OF PROFESSOR HOLLIS R. LYNCH OF COLUMBIA UNI-
VERSITY.

PREFACE

As this book appears in a series edited by Professor Hollis Lynch, I must begin by thanking him for asking me to write a life of Africanus Horton, whom I have been thinking about for many years. I am grateful for help from Major-General A. MacLennan who gave me access to Horton documents that I had never heard of, to Edward Dixon who let me use information he had collected for his own research, and to Christopher Webb who located an obscure Horton pamphlet for me. It is also a pleasure for me to thank Mr. C. P. Finlayson, Keeper of Manuscripts, University of Edinburgh, Mr. Donald Simpson, Librarian of the Royal Commonwealth Society, Miss Rosemary Keen, Archivist of the Church Missionary Society, Mr. J. M. Akita, Director of the Ghana National Archives, Mrs. Christine Wright, Master and Registrar, and Mr. Reginald Clark, Law Librarian, of the Supreme Court of Sierra Leone, Mr. C. A. E. Johnson of the Registrar-General's Office, Freetown, the librarians of King's College, London, the Royal Geographical Society and the Royal College of Surgeons, and the staff at the Public Record Office and at the British Museum reading room and newspaper library for their friendly assistance.

It is an even greater pleasure to have the opportunity of recording in print my gratitude to several friends who have encouraged and helped me—to my colleague George Shepperson, whose encouragement has only been one of countless other kindnesses to me during our association at the University of Edinburgh, to John and Jeanne Peterson, John Hargreaves and Ayo Langley, and to two eminent Sierra Leone doctors, worthy up-

v

holders of the fine tradition which Horton started, Dr. M. C. F. Easmon, who has over the years immensely enriched my understanding of Sierra Leone history, and Dr. Davidson Nicol, who has found time amid a distinguished career of medical research and public service to write illuminatingly about his famous predecessor and to pass on some of his knowledge to me.

CHRISTOPHER FYFE
Centre of African Studies
University of Edinburgh

CONTENTS

vii

Map Design by David Lindroth

INTRODUCTION

JAMES AFRICANUS BEALE HORTON—his name proclaims his colour. An African born and reared in Africa, he qualified in Britain as a medical doctor in 1859. For twenty years he served as an officer of the British army in West Africa, rising to be head of the Army Medical Department in the colony where he served, and retiring with the rank of lieutenant-colonel. He published several books on political and medical subjects. Born at a period of time and in a place where it was possible for a talented African to rise, he died just as that period was ending. After his death the fog of the colonial era descended over Africa, enshrouding the memory of her distinguished sons in oblivion and diffusing the myth that a black man could achieve nothing except as the servant of a white master.

Horton's achievements and opinions were shaped by the unusual society he grew up in, the British colony of Sierra Leone in the middle decades of the nineteenth century. The norms and aspirations he was bred to were strikingly different from those prevalent in the rest of Africa, or in the communities of African descent across the Atlantic. The modern reader can neither understand him nor fully sympathize with him without some knowledge of his background. The first chapter of this book provides an introductory account of the society where he spent his early years, and of the other parts of West Africa where he subsequently worked.

His published output exceeded the entire published output produced during his lifetime by his contemporaries in British West Africa (this excepts the prolific Liberian writers Edward Blyden and Alexander Crummell). He wrote four medical books and three on political themes. His political books ranged over all the issues then important in coastal West Africa—political and economic development, education, and race. Nor were his interests purely theoretical: he was an important influence in the development of national consciousness in Ghana.

Yet he led a full professional life, practising as a doctor, carrying out his medical duties (which included several periods of active wartime service), and often acting as a magistrate or administrative officer. He had a passion for research, but lacked the facilities for working systematically. The wonder is that with so many routine distractions, working far from libraries or the stimulus of an academic environment, he was able to produce so much.

Theory for him was always allied to practice. As a young man he published a pamphlet on the geology of the Ahanta region of Ghana. Later in life he prospected for gold there, secured concessions, and helped to form mining and railway companies. Always concerned to promote economic development, when he retired from the army he founded a bank in Freetown to provide capital for African entrepreneurs. But an early death in 1883, when he was aged only forty-eight, cut short the many-sided career of this energetic quick-minded man. In his book *West African Countries and Peoples* he outlined a political blueprint for Sierra Leone as an independent constitutional monarchy. Who would have been better fitted than himself to fill the role of elected sovereign?

Nor was his interest confined to West Africa. *West African Countries and Peoples* is subtitled "A Vindication of the Negro Race." He always remembered that his life and writings demonstrated that peoples of African descent were as competent as anyone else to produce original creative work. In the words of an obituary notice written by one of his Sierra Leone countrymen,

> his lifework was to endeavour, not only by his writings, but by his everyday action, to vindicate his country and race from misconstruction and insult, and to improve and maintain the capacity and destiny of the Negro to play an independent and important part in the future history and well-being of the world.[1]

1. *West African Reporter,* Oct. 20, 1883. In accordance with American usage dates are cited in this book in the sequence of month, day, year.

AFRICANUS HORTON
1835–1883

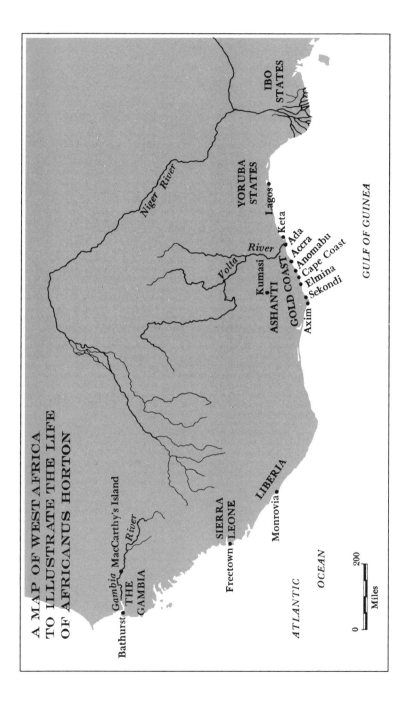

A MAP OF WEST AFRICA
TO ILLUSTRATE THE LIFE
OF AFRICANUS HORTON

THE GAMBIA

Bathurst

Gambia MacCarthy's Island

River

SIERRA
LEONE

Freetown

LIBERIA

Monrovia

Niger River

ASHANTI

Kumasi

Volta

River

GOLD COAST

Axim

Sekondi

Elmina

Cape Coast

Anomabu

Accra

Ada

Keta

YORUBA
STATES

Lagos

IBO
STATES

GULF OF GUINEA

ATLANTIC

OCEAN

0   200

Miles

I

THE WEST AFRICAN
BACKGROUND

SIERRA LEONE

THE SIERRA LEONE peninsula where Horton was born and bred, sticks out, small and mountainous, into the Atlantic Ocean. Its sharp wooded peaks overlook a wide estuary which forms a magnificent natural harbour. Long inhabited by the Bulom and Temne peoples, it attracted European ships once the Portuguese had begun venturing down the coast in the fifteenth century. Ships' captains would call in to trade, chiefly in slaves which were the main export commodity. European manufactures were supplied in return. Despite occasional quarrels, relations between Africans and Europeans tended to be peaceful. Each wanted the commodity the other supplied, and over the centuries they worked out established trading mechanisms. Only the wretched slaves suffered—exploited by their own countrymen who sold them, and by the strangers who bought them to carry across the Atlantic.

There were always people who cried out against the evil slave trade— the African victims, obviously, and a few African rulers. In Europe and America too, minority voices were raised in humanitarian protest. During the eighteenth century they were joined by those who disliked the slave trade for economic reasons, believing that slavery was a waste of economic resources, and that it would be better business to treat Africans as customers and sell them goods, rather than treat them as merchandise and sell them.

Then, as European technology developed, and the material gap between Europe and Africa widened, many Europeans came to feel that there was a moral gap between them too—that Europe represented "civilization" and Africa "barbarism." The slave trade made nonsense of such assumptions: civilized people do not openly buy and sell human beings. Hence it was possible by the 1780's to mount large, influential publicity campaigns in Britain and America which won widespread support and eventually succeeded in having the slave trade declared illegal.

The sponsors of British settlement in Sierra Leone were closely associated with the movement against the slave trade. The first settlers, who arrived there in 1787, were mostly Afro-Americans, former slaves who had served in the British army during the war of American independence and had made their way as free men to London. From there they were sent to found a new home of their own in Africa. Their community was short-lived. Many died during the initial rainy season. The survivors quarrelled with the neighbouring Temne, who burnt their town and dispersed them.

Members of the anti-slave trade lobby in London then founded a trading company, the Sierra Leone Company, to revive the settlement. They proposed to run it as a commercial venture, where trade in vegetable produce would be substituted for trade in slaves. About a thousand more former American slaves were brought over from Nova Scotia as settlers. Ostensibly free in Nova Scotia, they still felt vulnerable there, and were ready to emigrate to a new life as free people, on the continent from which they or their ancestors had been brutally carried away as slaves.

These "Nova Scotians" were good settlers. They had already displayed their resourcefulness in escaping from slavery and making new lives for themselves. They imported a pioneer tradition. Freetown, as their town was named, had a transatlantic look, with wide parallel streets and wooden frame-built houses and churches, like the pioneer towns in contemporary North America. Most of them had pioneer skills, many were literate. Already in Nova Scotia they had organized themselves into religious congregations, which remained their basic communal units. Their pastors were their leaders. Their vocabulary, norms, and aspirations were those of convinced Protestant Christians.

It had been imagined that they would form a community of farmers. But the country round Freetown was unsuited for more than subsistence farming. Those who wanted to make profits became traders. They invested their trading profits in building houses, often letting them to Europeans to bring in a regular income from rents. In all these ways the Nova Scotian settlers established a pattern of life for the world that Horton was to grow up in.

The Sierra Leone Company allowed them a share in local government, but all important policy decisions were made in London and executed by the Company's officials. In Sierra Leone, as in America, it was assumed that authority must be ultimately in white hands. This the settlers resented. Having escaped from slavery and exploitation, they were quick to notice anything that seemed to threaten their new free status. The Company's directors and officials found it hard to understand their suspicions, and tended to answer their complaints rigidly and unsympathetically. In 1800 a group of extremists among the settlers tried to take power themselves. Fighting broke out, only ended by the unexpected arrival of a shipload of new settlers with British troops on board.

These new settlers were Maroons—members of a community of African descent who had established themselves in the mountains of Jamaica. After making unsuccessful war against the Jamaican government, about 500 of them were deported, and eventually sent to Sierra Leone. At first they and the Nova Scotians were hostile. In time they fused into a more or less homogeneous settler community with a common way of life.

As well as antagonizing their own settlers, the Company's government antagonized the neighbouring Temne. When the original settlement was founded the Temne rulers had assented to a treaty (which they could not read) renouncing full sovereignty over the land granted to the settlers. This was against all usage. Normally land was only let to Europeans in return for rent, and not alienated permanently. But though the Temne maintained that they had never meant to alienate land, the Company held them to the letter of the treaty. In 1801 and 1802 Temne armies attacked Freetown, to drive the settlers away. But their attacks failed. Instead the Temne were themselves driven away, and much of the peninsula was left uninhabited.

The Company's hopes of making a profit out of the settlement were disappointed. War broke out between Britain and France in 1793, and their trade was irrevocably damaged. By the beginning of the century it was only kept going by subsidies from the British government. In 1808 the government took over the settlement altogether as a British colony and the Company was wound up.

At this period Protestant missionary societies were springing up in Europe and America with the aim of preaching the Christian gospel to all mankind. Catholic missions revived too. Protestant and Catholic alike preached Christianity in a European form—which assumed, for instance, that the ancient Christian churches of Egypt and Ethiopia were "debased." The Africans they converted to Christianity were expected to adopt European values, moral standards, and ways of life.

Sierra Leone was from the start a Christian colony, with a Christian settler population. In 1804 the newly founded Church Missionary Society, an evangelical society of the Church of England (its name usually abbreviated to C.M.S.), sent its first agents to Freetown. Methodist missionaries followed.

The British government continued the Company's anti-slave trade policy. The British Parliament declared the slave trade illegal in 1807, and Freetown became a base to enforce the laws against it. A naval squadron was sent to cruise along the coast, to intercept slave ships and bring them to Freetown for adjudication in the law-courts.

Despite this enforcement apparatus, the slave trade continued virtually unchecked for decades. Brazil and Cuba were being developed intensively for sugar production and slaves were in great demand. So long as large profits could be made, the slave trade continued. The naval squadron, cruising along hundreds of miles of coast, could be easily eluded. Dozens of ships might be captured but hundreds got through the ineffective blockade. Not until the 1860's was the transatlantic slave trade brought to an end.

Beginning 1808, then, year after year, hundreds (in some years

thousands) of people were landed from slave ships in Freetown
harbour to start a new life. By 1811 they already outnumbered
the Nova Scotian and Maroon settlers. These recaptives ("Liberated Africans" they were officially called) came from homelands thousands of miles apart, stretching from Senegal in the
north to the Congo in the south. Some even came from East
Africa, shipped through Mozambique. Most were Yoruba (from
the western part of the modern Nigeria). The next largest group
were Ibo (Horton's parents were Ibo), shipped from the Niger
Delta.

The British government sent out a governor and officials to
rule Sierra Leone, under the remote supervision of the Secretary
of State for the Colonies in London. In the days of sailing-ships
governors were under little control and could make decisions
much as they chose. It was for them to decide how to integrate
the recaptives into the population.

From 1814 to 1824 Sierra Leone was governed by a visionary
genius (rare among British colonial governors), Sir Charles
MacCarthy. Inspired by the prevalent desire to introduce "civilization" into Africa, he saw the recaptives as a means to fulfil his
vision. He proposed that government and missionaries cooperate,
to transform them into a Christian people, who would eventually
spread Christianity and European ways throughout West Africa.

He arranged for recaptives to be sent in small groups to build
villages in the deserted countryside round Freetown under the
supervision of C.M.S. missionaries. Some were settled by the sea-
shore; others went up to the mountains (Gloucester village, where
Horton was born, was in the mountains). The villages were to be
built like an English village, round a nucleus of parish church,
parsonage, and schoolhouse, with the houses spaced out along
tidy streets. Here, it was hoped, the recaptives and their children
would develop under missionary guidance into Christian communities.

The C.M.S. found it difficult to recruit missionaries. The very
concept of Christian missions, which later in the nineteenth
century was to become a central part of the Christian churches,
was still unfamiliar. Some of the first agents had to be recruited
in Germany. There were seldom as many as a dozen of them

active in the Colony, often much less. A missionary, with his wife if he had one, was usually on his own among his recaptive flock. He would look after their needs, settle disputes, treat the sick (for many arrived broken in health from the slave ships), and help them to adjust to life in a strange land.

This gave the missionary a close personal relationship with his distressed people, who were recovering from the hideous traumatic shock of the slave ship experience, and were in real need of help. It was something very different from the relationships established in other parts of Africa, later in the century, by the agents of the by then large institutionalized missionary societies, who were often forcing themselves upon people who did not want them.

In any case it was easier in the early nineteenth century for white missionaries to make friends with their people, than it was later on, when racial theories had grown increasingly prevalent. These first Sierra Leone missionaries were genuinely concerned to encourage their converts. They wanted to turn them into self-reliant Christians who would take charge of their own affairs. They were not trying, like many later missionaries, to keep them in perpetual tutelage, in the belief that Africans were incapable of anything better. Though paternalists, theirs was the paternalism of a father who knows that his "children" are going to grow up, not that of a master who wants to keep his subordinates in permanent subjection.

The missionaries were government officers and could exert secular authority over the villagers. At first they forced them to attend religious worship. But before long coercive authority could be relaxed, for the recaptives began to respond willingly. Lacking a common language, they adopted English. Cut off from the religions of their homelands, they listened with interest to Christian preaching, which invited them into a new life of salvation to match their new life of freedom. They took European names, usually the name of a missionary, or a prominent official or settler. They began wearing European-style clothes as an outward mark of their new status. Some adopted new skills and learnt to read and write—or at least saw to it that their children learnt.

As well as Europeans, the recaptives had the Nova Scotian settlers to look to for enlightenment. Not all of them went to the villages. Many stayed in Freetown working as servants in European or settler households. The settlers, who constituted a black Christian community living in European style, formed a reference group for them to copy. Many of them preferred to attend the settler churches. There they could see that Christianity was not merely a white man's religion. Some of the black settler pastors had congregations of their own in the villages: missionary activity was not confined to the white employees of societies in London.

Recaptives also helped one another to adjust to new ways. Those just landed from the slave ship were often sent to live with people from their own country who could instruct and help them until they could stand on their own feet. Hence within a decade of MacCarthy's death it was possible to describe the recaptives, with perhaps some exaggeration, as "a nation of free black Christians"[1]—willing converts to a new religion and a new way of life.

A mission so understaffed had to train up its own assistants. A Christian Institution was founded in 1814 to train teachers and future missionaries: this fitted MacCarthy's dream of using recaptives as a force to transform West Africa. After various vicissitudes it was moved in 1827 to Fourah Bay on the waterfront east of Freetown. From this institution, which Horton was to attend, grew Fourah Bay College, and ultimately the University of Sierra Leone. One of its first pupils, Ajayi Crowther, a young Yoruba recaptive, later became a minister, then a bishop, of the Church of England.

MacCarthy's policy did not always turn out as he intended. Like many visionaries, he was more interested in broad views than in details. The village churches he planned, with their massive Gothic towers, were erected by inexperienced recaptive masons and often collapsed. Large sums of money were spent importing equipment for the recaptives which rotted unused in

1. Public Record Office [hereafter cited as P.R.O.], C.O. 267/123, Temple 53, June 10, 1834.

the government stores or was stolen. Nor could the C.M.S. supply enough agents. The incidence of sickness and mortality was high: of 70 sent out between 1804 and 1824, 38 died, 7 went home ill. Laymen took charge of the villages instead, or the villages were left unsupervised and the people looked after themselves.

Thrown on their own resources in an unfamiliar environment, the recaptives began creating their own institutions of local government, based on what they had known in their homelands. The national groups in each village (Yoruba, Ibo, Congo, etc.) elected their own headmen, and formed benefit societies which also served as a means of settling disputes among members. Gradually the government withdrew official supervision from the villages, leaving the people to manage their own affairs. Thus the villages developed as peaceable, law-abiding communities whose inhabitants respected their own institutions.

They also respected the laws of the Colony. As British subjects they had the rights and privileges of free Englishmen. This was explicitly declared in 1829 by the Chief Justice of the Colony (in Langley's case) when he awarded an Ibo recaptive damages against a European official who had assaulted him. Henceforth recaptives could look to the law-courts for protection. They were in any case inclined to feel grateful towards those who had liberated them from slavery and had given them the opportunity of leading a new life.

Government, therefore, did not appear to them as a machine of colonial repression. They did not feel themselves in a "colonial situation." They identified with their British rulers, and felt the same kind of basic loyalty to the British crown that Englishmen felt in England.

This basic loyalty runs counter to what is usually perceived as the current of African nationalism. It has been interpreted as servile acceptance of a colonial master. But Sierra Leoneans were no more servile in their attachment to the British crown than were their white contemporaries in Canada or Australia. Like the Canadians and Australians they were proud of their place as free citizens of the British Empire.

These feelings were voiced years later, in 1890, by a Sierra Leone journalist—

We feel that of all the peoples in the British possessions none can be more loyal than the people of Sierra Leone. And why? Because we are not a conquered people like the Indians and others who must now and then think of revenge or of recovering their national power, . . . but we are a people born and fostered as it were by the British Nation whom we regard and own as our parents and to whom we look for instruction, advice, guidance and advancement in the same manner as other British subjects born in England.[2]

Horton's political writings can only make sense to those who understand that he grew up at a time and in an environment where loyalty to the British crown did not imply servility or self-hatred, but pride and self-respect.

Proud of their new status, preached to by Protestant missionaries who expounded a doctrine of thrift, industry, and self-help (the nineteenth-century Christian gospel of Hard Work), the recaptives sought opportunities to prove their worth and rise in the world. Like the Nova Scotians, they found that farming brought only meagre rewards. Like them, they turned to trade. As Europe industrialized, there was a growing demand there for lubricants and edible oils. Groundnuts (peanuts), from which oil can be extracted, grew plentifully in the northern part of the Colony's hinterland. Palm trees providing a glutinous palm oil and a fine palm kernel oil grew plentifully in the southern part. Enterprising recaptives, following a trail already opened by Nova Scotians and Europeans, moved inland to trade manufactured goods for vegetable produce. Others took to retail trade in Freetown—first hawking goods through the streets, then putting up a stall, finally building their own store. By the 1840's they were moving into the import-export trade, ordering goods from Britain and remitting produce in return.

They had little competition to face. The few European traders in Freetown were mostly small operators like themselves. Export firms in London or Manchester, flooded with goods from the expanding factories of mid-nineteenth-century Britain, were glad to extend their market outlets and deal with them. Like the Nova Scotians before them, prospering recaptives put their profits into house property, building substantial mansions and importing

2. *Sierra Leone Weekly News,* May 10, 1890.

fittings and furniture from Europe—gilt-framed mirrors, chandeliers, marble busts of Queen Victoria (a favorite ornament of a wealthy Freetown home). Thus within a few decades of landing naked and penniless from the slave ships, they were turning themselves into an affluent bourgeoisie in the style of their bourgeois contemporaries in Europe and America.

Having risen in the world themselves, they wanted their children to rise higher. Those who could afford it sent them to be educated in Britain. In 1845 the C.M.S. opened a grammar school in Freetown to provide secondary education for the sons of the rising bourgeoisie. A similar school for girls was opened in 1849.

Nevertheless, they were not merely a community of "Black Englishmen." With their feelings of gratitude and loyalty to their colonial mentors they still felt what the Nigerian historian E. A. Ayandele has called "a sense of separateness."[3] They retained their own forms of local government, their clubs and societies, their songs and dances, and many family customs. When they were sick, many preferred to go to a "country doctor" who treated them with familiar African remedies. Elements from African religions, like protracted burial ceremonies, or communicating with the family dead, were grafted unobtrusively onto Christian worship. Some still went on practising the religions of their homelands, though by mid-nineteenth century those who did so tended to worship in private, conscious that they were performing rites that were no longer socially acceptable.

The recaptives' children, born (like Horton) in Sierra Leone, were known as "Creoles," a distinctive name for a distinctive people with their own distinctive life-style. They evolved their own speech-form, "Krio," which seems to have been already in use by the 1850's—a blend of the lingua franca of coastal West Africa that had developed during the centuries of the slave trade (incorporating Portuguese, French, and English words and idioms) with the African languages of the recaptives' own homelands.

The Creole community therefore looked to two different cultural heritages—British and African. The professional elite that

3. E. A. Ayandele, *Holy Johnson* (London, 1970), 43.

emerged in Horton's generation was often inclined to stress its Britishness. Its members were embarrassed by traditional customs and might punish their children if they heard them speaking Krio. Horton compared Krio (or "Noang," as he called it) with London Cockney.[4] But they could not eradicate deep rooted ways, nor put down a language which was, as Edward Blyden described it, "the language of the domestic life, of courtship, of marriage, of death, of intensest joy and deepest grief."[5] Horton's Creole contemporary, Bishop James Johnson, who cherished above all the African elements in their culture, even advocated the use of Krio in schools, because it was "a thoroughly African language." Horton too, anxious though he was to learn everything useful that Europe had to teach, was still tenaciously proud of his African identity.

GHANA

Horton's professional career took him outside Sierra Leone to other parts of West Africa. He spent most of his active life in coastal Ghana, and played an important part in its history. The coastal region, known in his day as the Gold Coast, was then divided into many small states within three large language groups. On the west were the Akan peoples, who extended some 300 miles inland. East of them, on the Accra plains, were a smaller group, the Ga, and beyond them were the Ewe.

Some of the Akan peoples had for many centuries been working the rich gold deposits in their country, washing gold from the soil or hacking it out of gold-bearing rock. They exchanged the gold with Muslim African traders from the cities of the middle Niger in return for manufactured goods. Eventually much of it was carried across the Sahara to Mediterranean Africa and exported to far-off Europe and Asia—indeed, during the European Middle Ages Europeans relied on gold supplied by the distant Akan.

4. Quoted in T. J. Thompson, *The Jubilee and Centenary Volume of Fourah Bay College* (Freetown, 1930), 55.
5. Edward W. Blyden, *Christianity, Islam and the Negro Race* (London, 1887), 244.

Portuguese seeking a sea-route to the gold mines reached the coast in the 1480's. The rulers of the coastal Fanti (one of the Akan peoples) let them build a trading post which became known as Elmina. Other Europeans followed to buy gold—also slaves for the transatlantic market. They fortified their trading posts with thick walls in the style of the castles of mediaeval Europe. But these forts were not colonies. As in the Sierra Leone area during the slave trading era, land was not alienated. The European occupiers had to pay rent to African owners who retained sovereignty. At regular intervals the African landlord presented a "note" to the white tenant who paid him the rent due. During the course of wars or power struggles between African rulers the notes might pass from one landlord to another—but whoever held the note was entitled to receive the rent.

The Europeans, too, fought their little wars and captured the forts from one another. By the late eighteenth century only three groups were left—British, Danish, and Dutch. As the forts were not colonies they did not need to be clustered together in coherent areas. Each was sited where trade was best, jostling the neighbouring forts if need be. At Accra, for instance, British, Danish, and Dutch forts adjoined one another.

Though the Fanti and Ga usually sited their political capitals inland, away from direct European influence, trade towns grew up round the forts, where African traders congregated to do business with the Europeans. Each depended on the other for their trading commodities—the Africans receiving imported manufactures, the Europeans receiving slaves and gold. As a literate Fanti who visited England in the early eighteenth century put it, "the English live by us, and we by them."[6] It was therefore in the interests of both to be closely associated, not only by friendship but by kinship. Many Europeans married African wives. Even if they had white wives at home, these marriages were valid by the laws of the polygamous country they lived in. In this way they established close trading ties with their wives' families.

As the Europeans became partly Africanized, the Africans became partly Europeanized. Some Africans even became highly

6. Quoted in Margaret Priestley, *West African Trade and Coast Society*, (London, 1969), 39.

Europeanized, like William Amo who was taken to Germany as a boy, studied European philosophy, and eventually taught it at several German universities. At Cape Coast Castle, the main British fort, the Reverend Philip Quaque, a Fanti educated in England, officiated as chaplain from 1776 to 1816 and kept a school for Eurafrican and African children. There were similar schools in the Danish and Dutch forts. Horton, writing years later, was to contrast these schools favourably with what he felt was the inferior schooling being provided in his day in the government schools.

Those who had received a European-style education and were equipped with the advantages of literacy, could find employment as clerks or business agents. They formed a small elite, proud of their skills, and conscious of what they considered their social as well as educational prestige. Sometimes their pretensions brought them into conflict with the Fanti or Ga governments. Nevertheless, they remained part of Fanti or Ga society—unlike the Sierra Leone Creoles who had been cut off geographically from their homelands. Even the children of Europeans, in these matrilineal societies, usually identified with the families of their African mothers.

The landlords of the coastal forts preserved a jealous monopoly of export trade. Traders from inland were only allowed to deal with Europeans indirectly, through coastal middlemen who charged them commission. The inland peoples resented the coastal monopoly and tried to break it. From the late seventeenth century a group of Akan, living inland across the region which connected the trade northward to the Niger with the trade southward to the coast, united as the kingdom of Ashanti and gradually dominated their neighbours. In 1806 they began a series of successful military campaigns against the Fanti which gained them control of the coastal forts.

The Europeans in the forts were not directly affected by the Ashanti conquest, which merely provided them with a new landlord. But they were closely concerned with African politics, and were also rivals among themselves. The British tended to support the Fanti; the Dutch preferred the Ashanti. Some of the British traders at Cape Coast Castle began intriguing against their new Ashanti landlords. When Governor MacCarthy arrived in 1824 from Sierra Leone they persuaded him to intervene militarily in African politics in a way never attempted by Europeans before. At their prompting (for he knew nothing of the situation himself) he formed a coalition with the Fanti and the Danes and led out an army against the Ashanti.

This first aggression by British arms against a West African opponent ended in ignominious defeat. The army was almost annihilated. MacCarthy was killed and his head carried off to Kumasi, where it is still preserved. Eventually, however, British reinforcements arrived and defeated the Ashanti who agreed to withdraw again inland and give up their claim to the British and Danish forts. But they were still landlords for Elmina, which was occupied by their allies the Dutch.

After the Danish, British, and Dutch governments successively declared the slave trade illegal, the forts lost much of their economic value. The slave trade moved away. Gold and some ivory were still exported, and a small trade in palm oil grew up. But until the development of cocoa-farming at the end of the nineteenth century coastal Ghana was an economic backwater of little interest in Europe. In 1827 the British government even gave up all official responsibility for the forts, and for the next sixteen years they were controlled by the British traders who were settled there. Eventually, in 1843, however, government control was resumed.

When the Ashanti gave up the British and Danish forts, they gave up the right to receive rent. As there was no longer an African landlord, sovereignty passed, by implication, to the British and Danish occupiers. It could therefore be assumed that the forts were now British and Danish colonies.

Once established as sovereign rulers, the British traders began extending their influence from the tiny forts over their Fanti and Ga neighbours. In 1844 they persuaded the coastal rulers to agree to a "Bond"—a loose alliance which also gave British officials the right to sit as assistant judges in African courts to hear certain specified types of cases. In this way British influence was tentatively insinuated into the independent coastal states, and the way was opened for further political expansion.

THE GAMBIA

Horton also worked north of Sierra Leone in the Gambia Colony. British traders had operated along the Gambia river since the seventeenth century. In 1816 Governor MacCarthy established a British settlement, which he named Bathurst, on an island near the river mouth. Here, as in Sierra Leone, the ruler was deluded into accepting a treaty by which he inadvertently gave up sovereignty: hence it was a British colony. Recaptives were sent from Freetown to settle there, and it became a trading centre. Sovereignty was also obtained over an island 150 miles up the river, which was renamed MacCarthy's Island. Here too Horton was to work. In this way a British claim to the whole lower course of the river was asserted.

THE COAST

In the early nineteenth century formal empire was losing its charms in Britain. As British manufactures were in demand all over the world, there was no need for British colonies as marketing bases. There was little public interest in the small West African colonies. Most British people saw them as disease-ridden death traps, of only marginal economic value, which were hardly worth keeping, and might better be given up altogether.

The dynamic, expansive element in British West Africa during Horton's lifetime was not inspired from London: it was provided by the Sierra Leone Creoles. The tiny Sierra Leone peninsula and its hinterland only offered limited scope for their enterprise and ambitions. In 1839 a group of Yoruba recaptives in Freetown bought a ship and sailed back to the coast from which they had once been shipped. On their return to Freetown, they drew up a petition asking the government to found a British colony in the Yoruba country. The government refused to extend its responsibilities, but it did not stop them going back there themselves if they wanted to. Hundreds streamed down the coast, returning as prospering British citizens, in European suits and dresses, to the land from which they had once been

ignominiously dragged naked as slaves. At their invitation the
C.M.S. opened a mission at Abeokuta. Its first missionaries included Ajayi Crowther, who returned as a Christian pastor to the
town from which he had been captured and sold as a boy.

Opportunities awaited literate and skilled Sierra Leoneans all
along the coast—as government employees, as teachers or missionaries, as builders and carpenters, or in trade. Enterprising men
and women—many Creole women traded independently from
their husbands—would leave their homes in Freetown or the
Colony villages to seek their fortunes elsewhere, bringing with
them and disseminating all along the coast, the new ideas and
ways of life they had acquired.

Another, much smaller, expansive British element in West
Africa was represented by the successive British consuls stationed in the country round the Bight of Benin. Sent there to
help to detect slave ships, they tended to see themselves as empire builders, urging expansion on an unwilling government in
London. In 1861, at the consul's prompting, the town and island
of Lagos were annexed—a fourth little British West African
colony.

Lagos, a flourishing trading centre, had already attracted immigrants from Sierra Leone, and had a substantial Creole population. Here, as in Freetown and Bathurst, they invested their
profits in land, and built houses to provide an income from rents
for themselves and their families.

When therefore Horton travelled along the coast in the 1860's
and 1870's he found his own people wherever he went. Everywhere he was likely to find a welcome from men and women with
a background like his own—literate, enterprising Creoles, proud
of their distinctive life-style. Whether he was on MacCarthy's Island 150 miles up the Gambia river, or in Lagos, over a thousand
miles by sea from Freetown, the chances were that he might
recognize in the pastor, the magistrate, the postmaster, the shoe-
maker, the salesman, or the policeman, some half-remembered
face from his schooldays long ago in Gloucester village.

II

HORTON'S YOUTH
AND EDUCATION

VILLAGE BOYHOOD

GLOUCESTER VILLAGE, Horton's birthplace, hides in a long secluded valley, high among the mountains that tower above Freetown. Streams flowing down the steep slopes bring it water and a
fertile soil. Thick woodlands shelter it on all sides. Yet, shut in
from the world though it is, the eye may still catch through the
foliage, glimpses of the wide estuary and the low lying Bulom
Shore to the north, or the glittering prospect to the east, where
the sun shines on distant palm trees and half hidden waterways,
and the immense African continent seems to unfold endlessly, the
flat plain broken in the far distance by mountain ranges. Well
might Horton write that the peninsula where he was born "presents the most picturesque and lovely scenery that ever eye be-
held in a tropical world."[1]

Here, amidst what was then thick bush, a little group of recaptives was sent in 1814. Governor MacCarthy named their settlement Gloucester, after a member of the British royal family. A
royal name did nothing to help the miserable inhabitants,
planted down in a strange land, many of them sick with dysentery and ulcers from their fearful ordeal on board the slave ship.
But a kindly German missionary, the Reverend Henry Düring,

1. James Africanus B. Horton, *The Medical Topography of the West Coast
of Africa* (London, 1859), 10.

and his wife, came to live among them. He later described his depressing labours—trying to encourage a sickly, apathetic community to build houses, grow food, and make a new life for themselves.[2] Most of them could understand nothing he said—could not even understand one another, for about a dozen different African nationalities were represented. All were suspicious of him, afraid that he was only waiting to sell them back into slavery.

Gradually he won their confidence and persuaded them to build houses and wear the unfamiliar clothes provided for them. Every day he conducted morning and evening prayer and made them attend. At first they were angry. But as they learnt to understand him they began attending more willingly—some with enthusiasm. He began baptizing them. They built a large stone church with a massive square tower in the Gothic style MacCarthy approved of. A bell, a clock, and a barrel organ, all sent from England, were installed. At the formal opening in 1820 over 400 neatly dressed recaptives took part in the service. They built him a stone parsonage, a school house, and premises where the newly landed recaptives sent up from Freetown could be sheltered. When the Dürings left in 1823 after seven years at Gloucester (they died at sea on their way home), they could look back on a transformation that seemed to them almost miraculous.

Düring's purely material legacy was short lived. The church tower cracked and had to be demolished (though the bell survived for many generations). The walls were then struck by lightning and the church was abandoned for some years. Religious services had to be held in a thatched hut. But his main achievement remained—an African Christian community.

During the decade after his death few Europeans remained long at Gloucester. They died or were invalided or were transferred. Continuity in the task he had begun was provided by recaptive teachers who ran the school, particularly by John Bartholomew and Matthew Harding. Bartholomew came from the Nupe country of modern Nigeria, and had been shipped as a slave on the same ship as the future Bishop Crowther. Harding was from the Gola country of the modern Liberia. Twice en-

2. C.M.S. Archives [hereafter C.M.S.], CAI/089, Memoir of the Reverend Henry Düring, Nov. 1822.

slaved, but twice freed, he was one of the first villagers at Gloucester and one of Düring's first converts. In 1826, when all the Europeans had died or been invalided, he took charge of the village, and remained there ten years helping and instructing succeeding missionaries.

Recaptive village life was centred round the societies, or "companies," formed by the villagers. Many missionaries were suspicious of them, fearing that the members went on practising non-Christian religious rites at the meetings. Harding had the idea of forming a "Church Company," a benefit society whose members would be obligated to one another in familiar ways, but with specifically Christian rites. After leaving Gloucester he started similar societies elsewhere. He retired from work in 1852, but lived on, a historic link with the Colony's past, until 1894, outliving Horton by eleven years.

Bartholomew and Harding were not men of advanced education, but their surviving letters and journals in the C.M.S. archives in London show that they were literate and intelligent, plainly capable of instructing children. They and the other recaptive teachers, men and women, employed in the village schools, worked under the supervision of conscientious missionaries, some of whom were men of real scholarship. The Reverend James Schön and the Reverend C. F. Schlenker, for instance, both of whom worked for a while at Gloucester during the 1830's, were distinguished pioneers in African linguistic research. These European and African teachers took their work seriously. They encouraged the children to be diligent, ambitious, achievement-oriented Christians. Hence the children of Gloucester and the other villages had the chance of a better education than many white children in contemporary rural England—who were merely being trained to take a docile, subordinate place in a stratified society.

By 1835, the year Horton was born, Gloucester could plausibly be called a Christian village. Some villagers kept up their old forms of worship, but attachment to them was waning. Most went regularly to church—some no doubt as a social formality, some out of piety. No one worked openly on Sundays. Everyday speech was filled with religious phrases, and the Christian religion set the norms of conduct.

Careful censuses were taken in the Colony in 1831 and 1833.[3] They showed Gloucester as a village of about 800 inhabitants, laid out in seven streets. As with many censuses, the data are not always consistent, but the second shows 72 families living in timber-framed houses, the rest in mud and wattle huts. Most of the inhabitants had European names. Some had skilled trades; they were carpenters, sawyers, tailors, and shoemakers. But there was not enough work to employ them all in the village. Many went down every day to Freetown to work, or to take their vegetables to market, returning in the evening up the steep and rugged pathway through the woods to their quiet village.

In 1833 census includes the names of James Horton, carpenter, and his wife Nancy. Both were of Ibo origin. Their son once declared himself to be "descended from the royal blood of Isuama Eboe."[4] Whatever their claims to royal descent, they came from a people noted for energy, ambition, and individualism—characteristics appropriate for Sierra Leone recaptives at this period.

The name "Horton" was derived from an English missionary who was in Sierra Leone from 1816 to 1821. But it does not neccessarily follow that James Horton was in the Colony by 1821: he might have arrived later and adopted the name secondhand from anoher recaptive, as often happened. When he died in 1867 his age was given as seventy-six,[5] so he must have been enslaved and recaptured as a grown man. In later life he had some correspondence with the secretary of the C.M.S. in London. It is not clear from the surviving letters whether he wrote them himself or had them written for him. Whether written or dictated, his compositions display the kind of fluent, conventional piety one would expect from an intelligent mission convert.

His son James was born on the 1st of June 1835, and spent the first twelve years of his life at Gloucester. During these years there was more continuous missionary supervision than in the previous decade. The church was rebuilt (and was still standing, after recent repair, in 1970). The missionary's house, a two-storied building by the church, was considered by an English

3. Returns bound up in P.R.O., C.O.267/111 (1831) and C.O.267/123 (1833).
4. James Africanus B. Horton, *Letters on the Political Condition of the Gold Coast* (London, 1870), ii.
5. *African Times,* June 22, 1867.

visitor to be more comfortable than the houses occupied by many of the poorer clergy in England.[6] These missionaries and their families will have been almost the only white people the young James Horton ever saw in the village. Few came up from Free-town—only occasional officials or passing visitors to the Colony. An emigration agent turned up at the village school in 1843 to try and persuade the boys to emigrate to the West Indies.[7] After 1847 even the European missionaries withdrew, leaving the vil-lage to Creole pastors. Henceforth it was an entirely African village, with its own local government, nominally supervised by the authorities in Freetown.

It was in that year, 1847, that James Horton left Gloucester. The Reverend James Beale, a C.M.S. missionary who had for-merly been stationed in the mountain villages, was recruiting boys from the village schools for the C.M.S. Grammar School in Freetown. Horton was among them. His father could not afford to pay the school fees, so he was given a scholarship, paid for by the Chief Justice of the Colony, John Carr, an Afro-Trinidadian who, during his twenty-five years as judge in Sierra Leone, sup-ported many boys at the Grammar School.

Even in the streets of Freetown Horton as a schoolboy did not see many white faces. In a population of about 15,000 not more than 150 were Europeans. Nor did their white skin necessarily confer high status. Some were sailors from passing ships, socially inferior to the black officials and shopkeepers. Nor did a black skin necessarily imply low status. Afro-West Indians like Judge Carr held many of the senior government posts, including some of the most senior—Colonial Secretary, head of the Customs de-partment, and legal adviser to the government.

Shortly before Horton entered the Grammar School, an Afro-West Indian, William Fergusson, had been governor. Born in Jamaica, he qualified as a doctor in Scotland at the University of Edinburgh, was commissioned as an officer in the British army, and served for many years in Sierra Leone, eventually as

6. T. E. Poole, *Life in Sierra Leone and the Gambia* (London, 1850), vol. i, p. 233.
7. Sierra Leone Archives, Liberated African Department Letterbook, Jan. 11, 1843; for the West Indian emigration policy, see Johnson U. Asiegbu, *Slavery and the Politics of Liberation, 1787-1861* (London, 1969).

governor, the only man of African descent who ever held that rank substantively. Horton, who was also to qualify at Edinburgh University, and to serve as an officer in the British army, could therefore look back on a distinguished black predecessor who had risen by his merits.

Colour was no bar to promotion in the society he grew up in. In Sierra Leone he was spared the anguish that would have tormented him had he been born in 1835 in the United States, to grow up in a society where white men always ruled and black always obeyed.

Even so, Freetown society was by no means wholly homogeneous. The Nova Scotian and Maroon settlers and their families, though a tiny group in the population, formed an exclusive social elite. They despised the recaptives, recalling how they had once seen them land naked and degraded from the slave ships. But their own superiority was built on a shaky economic foundation. The recaptives, pushing and enterprising, soon began elbowing the settlers out of trade, and supplanting them as leaders of the business community—even buying up property in central Freetown, which the settlers regarded as their own enclave.[8] There was also a division between the Colony people and those who came in from the surrounding country—at this period mostly Temne—to work in Freetown, where they were usually treated as inferiors. But this division did not become acute until later in the century, after Horton's death, when the interior was brought into closer contact with the Colony, and people began migrating to Freetown in large numbers. In his lifetime it was still overwhelmingly a Creole city.

EDUCATION IN FREETOWN

The C.M.S. Grammar School where Horton entered in May 1845[9] was modelled on similar institutions in England. About forty

8. See Arthur T. Porter, *Creoledom* (London, 1963); for Horton's own reaction to settler arrogance see p. 124 below.
9. His name is number 85 on the *Sierra Leone Grammar School Entrance Register, 1845-1935.* I am grateful to Professor John Hargreaves for providing me with a microfilm of it.

boys, grouped in four classes, were taught a curriculum which was largely classical and mathematical, with a strong religious emphasis. They boarded in the school, a three-storied building dating from Governor MacCarthy's days, which was too small to hold them in comfort; conditions improved in 1852 when a new wing was added. An English missionary-principal was in charge, assisted by Creole teachers and pupil-teachers.

The Reverend James Peyton, principal in Horton's time, was not content merely to teach. Like most contemporaries in England, he was deeply concerned with character-training and with supervising the boys' behaviour. Discipline was strict: serious offenders were locked up in solitary confinement until they showed adequate repentance. During Horton's second year two very competent Creole teachers were taken on—Daniel Carrol and James Quaker. Carrol subsequently gave up teaching for the government legal service. Quaker, who had been trained at the C.M.S. training institution in London, eventually became principal of the school. Under their care the boys were conscientiously but rigidly supervised.

Much of the teaching was organized synoptically. A class would take one geographical area (Ancient Greece or Asia, for example), and study it historically, politically, and geographically. Horton later followed this kind of approach in his books. During his time at the school Peyton went on leave for a year (Horton's benefactor, Beale, took temporary charge), and returned from England full of enthusiasm for practical education. He bought land for a cotton plantation, and made the boys plant and prepare cotton. He taught some of them land surveying, and gave lectures on elementary physics that Horton may later have found useful.[10]

In such a school, extra-curricular activities tended to have a religious bias. There were meetings to discuss such subjects as "the Melancholy Narrative of the Patagonian Missionaries." James Quaker organized debates on religious topics where prepared speeches were presented. Horton no doubt participated. He was never backward in airing his views.

10. C.M.S., CAI/0173, Quarterly Reports of the C.M.S. Grammar School.

Among the Grammar School records in the C.M.S. archives
there survives a list of subscribers to the new school building of
1852, chiefly government officials and Freetown shopkeepers.
Among them appears Horton's name with a donation of five
shillings. Here he was putting preaching into practice in a char-
acteristically uninhibited way, without troubling how others
might judge him—his schoolmates who might consider him sycophantic, the missionaries who might consider him presumptuous,
or the Freetown elite who might laugh at him.

In January 1853, with a good grounding in elementary Greek,
Latin, and mathematics, he was transferred to the Fourah Bay
institution to train for the ministry of the Church of England.
This was the obvious goal for an industrious young man from a
pious home with a strict religious education. Aged only seventeen, he was one of the youngest of the nineteen students, most
of whom were aged at least twenty.

Here the principal was a man very different from his previous
teachers. The Reverend Edward Jones was an Afro-American,
born in Charleston, South Carolina, of free parentage. He was
graduated in 1826 from Amherst College (he is believed to be
the first American college graduate of African descent), and was
ordained a minister of the Episcopal Church.[11] He then left the
United States to work in Africa. In America he had suffered the
bitter humiliations of life in a racist society. In Sierra Leone
during his early years he was persecuted by a half-crazy governor
before transferring from government to C.M.S. service. Though
relaxed and easygoing in his everyday manner, he was reserved
and sensitive, reacting sharply when roused. White colleagues
resented his outspoken opinions. He represented the heritage of
protest against racial oppression, otherwise almost absent from
the Colony at this time. Such a man opened his students' eyes to
a world beyond their little Creole homeland and that of their
white teachers in Europe.

At this time he took part in an expedition that Horton found
deeply moving. The Sierra Leone Yoruba having persuaded the
C.M.S. to found a mission in their homeland, the Sierra Leone

11. Hugh Hawkins, "Edward Jones: First American Negro College Graduate?"
in *School and Society*, Nov. 4, 1961.

Ibo (Horton's people) wanted to do the same. In 1853 Jones went down the coast for a few months with a group of Colony Ibo to investigate the prospects. Eventually a mission was founded at Onitsha on the Niger under the supervision of an Ibo missionary, the Reverend J. C. Taylor.

Fourah Bay College (as it came to be called) was housed in new premises, designed especially for the purpose. It was built east of Freetown, on what was then a secluded part of the shore. It belonged to the C.M.S. and was intended at this period chiefly for training pastors and missionaries. The first bishop of Sierra Leone, recently appointed from England, resided in the building. Jones expressed the hope that his presence might restrain the students' behaviour: "the native habit of loud speaking and making a noise in all their movements," he wrote, "is very hard to put down."[12]

The curriculum was primarily religious, but included mathematics, geography, and language study. The C.M.S. in Sierra Leone had a strong linguistic tradition: Horton just missed being taught by Sigismund Koelle, one of the most famous of all African language scholars, who left the College the year before he entered. Koelle was succeeded by another German linguist, the Reverend Charles Reichardt, who taught Hebrew and Arabic. Horton studied Hebrew (he was never in the Arabic class) and found a teacher of a kind he had not met before—not just a schoolmaster passing on secondhand information, but a research scholar who learnt and taught with pleasure. Reichardt's enthusiasm was reciprocated. When he fell ill, and then returned to work after a while, expecting to find his little Hebrew class— Horton and two others—had forgotten all he had taught them, he found to his delight that they had gone on working at Hebrew grammar by themselves.[13]

Here, as at the Grammar School, Horton was encouraged to take an interest in agriculture, for Reichardt enjoyed gardening. (The students helped him to lay out a coffee plantation at Fourah Bay, but it was too near the sea and the plants died.)[14] Horton

12. C.M.S., CAI/0129, Jones's report dated Oct. 31, 1854.
13. C.M.S., CAI/0182, Reichardt to the Reverend Henry Venn, Feb. 6, 1854.
14. Horton, *Medical Topography*, p. 18.

also learnt to record readings from a rain gauge. Otherwise his studies were concentrated on the Old Testament in Hebrew and the New Testament in Greek, and on mathematics, for which he showed a special aptitude. His mathematics teacher was a Creole pastor, the Reverend George Nicol, who, like himself, had grown up at Gloucester.

Jones was inclined to think well of Horton, finding him quick and promising. But he also found him (with implied disapproval) "somewhat mercurial in character," lacking in humility and steadiness—doubting perhaps whether a student so impulsive, quick-witted, and self-assertive would prove suited to the life of a village pastor for which he was being trained.

MEDICAL STUDENT

A journalistic description of Sierra Leone was published in 1836 with the eye-catching title *The White Man's Grave*. The Colony's bad reputation derived from the early days of settlement when, as in most pioneer settlements, sickness and death prevailed. Lurid tales of this era were repeated through succeeding generations by the Colony's many enemies. Europeans who resided there often felt differently. "Every European who has lived a length of time in Africa calls all parts of the coast unhealthy except the place where he happened to dwell," wrote Dr. Thomas Winterbottom, who spent four years in Sierra Leone—and then lived on in England until the age of ninety-four.[15] It seems to have been no more unhealthy for them than most parts of tropical Africa or the Caribbean, and healthier than Bengal.

But any tropical country was hazardous in an age when it was still not realized that "fevers" (as they were generically called) were mosquito-borne. Malaria was endemic. Yellow fever, a far more virulent, and usually fatal, mosquito-borne disease was also introduced from time to time. The settled population was immunized by childhood infection, which is much less serious, but it spread devastatingly among adult Europeans. Many kinds of intestinal diseases were also prevalent.

15. Thomas Winterbottom, *An Account of the Native Africans in the Neighbourhood of Sierra Leone* (London, 1803), vol. i, p. 180.

Malaria patients were sometimes treated with quinine, but it was not used generally as a prophylactic until after 1854, when Dr. William Baikie brought back the crew of his Niger Expedition unscathed after their daily drink of it. Some of the favoured treatments were as painful as the disease. Doctors observed that recovery was often accompanied by salivation, so they administered small doses of mercury which stimulates saliva. The miserable patient might lie for weeks in an agony of mercurial poisoning, with saliva drooling out of a mouth locked open in paralysis.[16]

Mortality and morbidity were always high in the British regiments serving in West Africa, and medical officers were no more immune than anyone else. To attract doctors into such an unattractive service, a double medical staff had to be maintained at great expense to give them regular leave to England. Even so, recruitment was difficult and the services provided were inadequate.

In 1853 the Deputy-Secretary at the War Office in London, Benjamin Hawes, who had previously been at the Colonial Office and therefore knew something about West Africa, proposed to remedy the deficiency by recruiting Africans. Recalling the successful career of Governor William Fergusson, he proposed that suitable young Africans be brought to England to study medicine and then be commissioned as army medical officers. The proposal was considered carefully, particularly its social implications. It was felt that the candidates must have a respectable educational and social background. One official minuted,

> They will, under any circumstances, have immense difficulties to contend with in the prejudice of this country against the Negro Race. As the sons of *Merchants* and treated by the Govt throughout as the sons of *Gentlemen* half these difficulties will be overcome.[17]

Early in 1854 it was decided to ask the C.M.S. to act as an intermediary, selecting suitable candidates and looking after them in England, the War Office refunding the expense. The C.M.S. London Committee agreed but did nothing. Over a year passed.

16. For a description, see P.R.O., Adm 101/88(3), Journal of Alexander Bryson, 1831-32.
17. P.R.O., W.O.43/91/23965; W.O.43/91/120001.

In July 1855 the War Office sent an impatient reminder. Then the C.M.S. secretary wrote hurriedly to Jones, telling him to choose three young men immediately and send them to England on the next boat.[18]

Jones immediately summoned the three best students of recent years. Two had already left and were working as catechists in country parishes. Samuel Campbell, the oldest, had been a favourite pupil of Koelle's. William Broughton Davies, another outstanding student, had been recommended to go to England to train for a teaching position on the College staff. Nevertheless, Jones felt the offer of a medical career was too valuable to pass over. The third was Horton, now aged twenty, and entering his final year. They assembled hastily at the College for early morning prayer, received a few words of exhortation and blessing, and next day were on the boat to England.[19]

They were not (in the words of the War Office minute) "sons of *Merchants*": their parents were manual labourers in the Colony villages. But they had grown up in an open-ended society where the talented could rise irrespective of colour. They had been well-educated in the classics of Greece and Rome, still at that period the standard intellectual feeding of an English gentleman, at institutions which aspired to mould manners and character along the lines approved of in middle-class England. With this grounding they could hope to be accepted, insofar as their colour permitted, on an equal level with other university students.

They were admitted to King's College in the University of London. The periods of study then prescribed for medical students in Britain varied considerably from one institution to another. At King's they could in three years take a medical qualification which would entitle them to practise. But it was felt desirable that they should in addition have a higher qualification. London University would not award a medical doctorate for less than six years' study. Edinburgh University, however, awarded a doctorate after four, three of which could be spent at King's. Horton, therefore, was to spend three years in London working

18. C.M.S., G/C.1, vol. 30, minutes of Feb. 21, 1854; July 17, 1855.
19. CAI/0129, Jones to Venn, Aug. 17, 1855; Report, Oct. 31, 1855.

for an M.R.C.S., (Membership of the Royal College of Surgeons) and a fourth in Edinburgh working for an M.D.

On arrival they went to the C.M.S. training institution at Islington in North London. But King's College and its associated hospital were in central London, inconveniently far off for daily travel on cold winter mornings. Nor was the routine of a theological college suited for medical students. So they moved into lodgings near King's College Hospital, the C.M.S. paying their expenses, which were refunded by the War Office.[20]

King's College had originally been founded as a specifically Church of England institution, which naturally recommended it to the C.M.S., and tended to be hampered by conservatism and timidity. It was impoverished and ill-equipped: "a general air of poverty and depression brooded over the dingy scene."[21] The hospital was small, and though a new wing was opened in 1857 it was still inadequate. Not until after Horton had left was it properly rebuilt. The teaching staff were overworked and underpaid. Nevertheless, they were determined to improve the quality of the teaching, and during the 1850's standards were raised. An important innovation made in Horton's time was the replacement of untrained, brutalized, and often drunken nurses with nurses trained to the high standards laid down by Florence Nightingale. Thus, despite its many deficiencies, it showed the students an example of the new type of disciplined efficient hospital.

Several of Horton's teachers were men of some medical distinction—two prominent surgeons, a pioneer medical statistician, and two distinguished botanists, who no doubt inspired him with his abiding interest in botany.[22] King's, despite its religious orthodoxy, also had a geological tradition: Sir Charles Lyell, one of the founders of modern geology, had once been a professor there. Geology was another of Horton's greatest interests. He

20. C.M.S., G/C.1, vol. 31, minutes of Oct. 8, 1855; Nov. 6, 1855.
21. F. J. C. Hearnshaw, *The Centenary History of King's College, London (1828-1929)* (London, 1929), 206.
22. See the entries in the *Dictionary of National Biography* under Richard Partridge, Sir William Fergusson, W. A. Guy, A. Henfrey, and J. F. Royle, all of whom taught Horton (names of Horton's teachers on Edinburgh University MS, "Medical Examinations, 1859, Horton").

arranged for samples of iron-bearing soil from the mountains near Gloucester to be sent to London for one of the professors to analyse.

The three African students were cared for in London by the Reverend Henry Venn, Honorary Secretary of the C.M.S. Venn was a rarity—a white man who could see Africans as equals. It may have been because as a child he had played with a group of African children sent over to London from Sierra Leone. During his thirty years with the C.M.S. he poured out letters of sympathy and understanding to the mission churches, urging angry European missionaries to be forbearing and charitable, comforting and encouraging their African victims.

Yet he was no impractical visionary, imagining that racial differences could be blown away by gusts of kindly goodwill. "Distinctions of race," he wrote, "are irrepressible."[23] He insisted, therefore, that the indigenous Christian populations of ' Africa and Asia must be allowed to build up churches of their own, African and Asian churches. The white missionary's task was to help them to build—and then when the church was built, pull out. Venn's affectionate guidance sustained many young Africans in a London that, if not actively hostile, was indifferent and insensitive. Horton came to regard him as a second father.

Venn had feared from the start that it might be unwise to bring them to England at the onset of winter. The cold, dirty London fogs were too much for Samuel Campbell. By the middle of the following year his health broke down and he had to be sent home; he died of bronchitis a few months after his return to Freetown. Davies suffered too in the cold climate, but came through all right. Horton's health seems to have been unaffected.

They had to work hard—fourteen hours a day, Horton recalled later[24]—to make up for their lack of pre-medical training. His hard work was rewarded, for he gained the prize in surgery and five certificates of honour in other branches of medical study. He joined the College medical society, which read and discussed

23. W. Knight, *The Missionary Secretariat of the Rev Henry Venn* (London, 1880), 285.
24. James Africanus B. Horton, *Physical and Medical Climate and Meteorology of the West Coast of Africa* (London, 1867), 68.

serious papers; in later life he described himself as a "Corresponding Member" of it. During his time there the society sponsored a student protest. Bodies for dissection were in short supply. Students were unable to get adequate practical experience, and they formed a committee to protest to the relevant professional and academic authorities.[25]

In April 1858 Horton and Davies passed the examination of the Royal College of Surgeons which admitted them to medical practice. The C.M.S. presented each of them with a five-guinea watch.[26] They were elected Associates of King's College, a distinction conferred on satisfactory graduates. Then they moved to Scotland, Horton to the University of Edinburgh, Davies to the University of St. Andrews, to qualify for doctorates.

Horton and Davies were a strikingly contrasting pair. Both had a similar upbringing. Davies was the son of a Yoruba farmer at Wellington, a village east of Freetown. But where Horton was self-assertive and impulsive, Davies was quiet and reserved, with a gentle, courteous manner. Plainly he would have fitted into the career they were both originally intended for—that of a peaceful man of religion—better than one can ever imagine Horton doing. Nevertheless, though a man of peace, he proved a good army officer, and when the need arose showed coolness and gallantry in the field. Like Horton, he was a competent, hard-working, self-sacrificing doctor.

Physically, too, they made a contrast. Davies was tall, with a dignified manner. Horton was small, inquisitive, and bustling. Always ready to assert himself, he now became concerned to assert his identity as an African. The testimonial he received from the principal of King's College was addressed to "James B. Horton"—for already in Sierra Leone he had adopted the middle name "Beale" after his missionary benefactor.[27] But in Edinburgh he registered as "James Africanus Beale Horton," a name that immediately established his continent of origin.

25. *Transactions of the Medical Society of King's College* (London, 1857-58), vol. ii, pp. 219-21.
26. C.M.S., G/C.1, vol. 32, minute of March 6, 1858.
27. There is a copy of the testimonial in C.M.S., CAI/0117 with Horton, Nov. 13, 1863; CAI/0129 Jones, Aug. 17, 1855, refers to him as "James B. Horton."

HORTON IN EDINBURGH

The University of Edinburgh in 1858 was no longer the pre-eminent institution it had been in the late eighteenth century, but it still attracted outstanding teachers. The four medical professors whose classes Horton attended were men of some distinction. He studied midwifery with one of the most famous medical men of his day—Sir James Young Simpson, who laid the foundation of modern gynaecology and was the first surgeon to use chloroform in operations. But the anatomy teacher Robert Knox, whose racial theories Horton was later to contest, had left Edinburgh for London two years earlier: had he remained and taught Horton he might have had to revise his belief in the innate incapacity of Negroes.[28]

Horton lodged at 50 Rankeillour Street (still standing in 1972), at the east end of a terrace below Arthur's Seat, not more than ten minutes' walk from his nine o'clock lectures on cold winter mornings. In Edinburgh, as in London, he seems not to have suffered from the chilly weather.

Edinburgh medical students had to qualify with a preliminary examination in Latin: Horton will have had no trouble translating short passages from Tacitus and Sallust, and one of Horace's best known odes. At the end of six months, in April 1859, he was examined orally in five medical subjects, and in June in eight more. All these he passed satisfactorily. In Practice of Medicine he was the only student of the year to be awarded Honours. He also wrote a doctoral thesis, for which he was commended, and (with nine others) he was awarded a certificate of merit for helping with histological demonstrations.[29]

His "Thesis on the Medical Topography of the West Coast of Africa including Sketches of its Botany" was in two parts. The

28. There are references to Horton's Edinburgh career in the manuscript volume "Medical Examinations, 1859," in the University of Edinburgh Library. I am grateful to Mr C. P. Finlayson, Keeper of Manuscripts, for his kindly assistance.

29. *Edinburgh University Calendar*, 1859-60, pp. 79, 90, 93.

first was "Topographical and Botanical Records," the second "The Seasons and Meteorology of West Africa." As his own experience of West Africa was limited to the Sierra Leone peninsula, much of what he wrote had to be extracted from the published works of others. But some of it (possibly even as much as half) was based on his own personal observations and recordings. He described many plants, obviously from his own experience, even assigning his name to a species he claimed to have identified, *Clerodendrum Hortonium*.

The thesis was written in a fluent style, embellished with a few classical quotations and a ponderous joke (writing of "musquitoes"—as he spelt it—"the inhabitants suffer from the surgical operation of phlebotomy, which these creatures though uninvited practise on them"). The examiners made no pencilled comments on the script, apart from correcting some of the botanical names. On the title page his name appeared in full, followed by "Native of West Africa."

A work on botany and meteorology might seem an unexpected offering for a medical thesis. But the title "Medical Topography" supplied the connexion. He assumed (and this assumption was to underlie all his later published works) that soil, vegetation, and climatic conditions directly affect human health. He claimed, for instance, that the blowing of the *harmattan* wind in West Africa "produces some peculiar physiological change in the system by which it is enabled to resist diseases even of the most malignant type." He postulated a connexion between heavy clay soil and malaria. Hence he saw his research as a necessary part of the study of tropical medicine.

At the University of St. Andrews degrees were given out more briskly than in Edinburgh. Davies was awarded his M.D. before 1858 was out, and came to stay in Edinburgh, though not in the same lodgings as Horton. While there he competed for a botanical essay (comparing the Linnean and Natural systems of classification) for which the Edinburgh professor of Botany awarded him an additional prize.

There were at least two black American students at Edinburgh University at this time, J. Ewing Glasgow and Robert M. Johnson, who concerned themselves with publicizing the abolitionist cause.[30] But during Horton's year there the abolitionist movement was in decline in Scotland—to be revived shortly after he left by a visit from Frederick Douglass. Neither here nor in London does Horton seem to have taken any part in abolitionist or humanitarian politics. Probably, as George Shepperson has suggested, he was too busy with his medical studies.[31]

But with their interest in botany he and Davies were elected foreign members of the Botanical Society of Edinburgh. He joined, and became president of, the Pathological Society of Edinburgh, and the Noetic Society of Edinburgh. Plainly he attached importance to his membership of these societies, for he added them after his name on the title pages of some of his books.[32]

ARMY OFFICER

During the nineteenth century professional men in Britain became increasingly concerned to establish their status on the basis of exclusive standards. In 1858 the medical profession won legal recognition. By act of Parliament all medical practitioners were obliged to register their qualifications: those who failed to do so were denied legal protection. Horton and Davies were therefore joining a profession that was rising in social esteem and professional competence. Davies, who graduated in 1858, appeared in the first edition of the *Medical Register*, which appeared in 1859; Horton appeared in 1860.

On 5 September 1859 they were commissioned as officers in the British army, for service in West Africa, with the rank of staff-assistant surgeon. The army medical service, like the medical profession generally, was being reorganized and raised to a higher standard at this time. Hitherto there had been no unified medical corps: medical officers were attached to regiments and had only supernumerary status. The medical disasters of the

30. I am grateful for the material in this paragraph to Edward Dixon.
31. George Shepperson, Introduction to Horton, *West African Countries,* 2nd ed., (Edinburgh, 1969), xi-xii.
32. I can trace no information about either.

Crimean War revealed the weakness of the system. A Royal Warrant of 1858 established a unified medical staff, with its own pay
and promotion scales. Medical officers were commissioned on
appointment as staff-assistant surgeons, ranking with lieutenants,
and, after six years' service, with captains. On promotion to the
next grade, surgeon-major, they ranked with majors, and after
twenty years of service, with lieutenant-colonels. Horton and
Davies therefore served with the status of regimental officers in
a branch of the service that was increasingly winning recognition.

Staff-assistant surgeons were paid 10 shillings a day (£182.10 a
year), rising to 11 shillings and sixpence after five years' service,
13 shillings after ten (£237.5 a year). These rates might seem
low at a time when it was reckoned that in civilian practice a
doctor could earn £300 after five years, £500 after ten. But army
doctors were spared the heavy expenses civilian practitioners
then had to incur (particularly, buying a practice). Accommoda-
tion was found for them and they received the allowances paid to
regimental officers. Life in West Africa was cheap—indeed most
of the regimental officers who served there were either too poor
to afford the expense of a good regiment or were in debt. They
could pick up additional income by acting in medical and administrative posts under the colonial government, which was
usually understaffed.

They could also practise privately. Horton regularly treated
civilians in the towns where he was stationed and charged them
fees: in a law case he brought in 1874 to recover unpaid fees,
he declared that fifteen guineas "was a very low charge indeed,
taking into consideration the position" of the patient's family.[33]
With all these sources of income he was able to make substantial
savings during his twenty years in the army.

Without delay he put his doctoral thesis into print. *The Medical Topography of the West Coast of Africa; with Sketches of its
Botany* was published in 1859 by John Churchill, a London pub-
lisher specializing in medical books. Apart from a few verbal
and stylistic changes and the addition of two long quotations

33. C.M.S., CAI/0117 enclosures in Horton, Nov. 13, 1863; Ghana National
Archives, S.C.T.5/4/44, p. 468 (case dated June 2, 1874).

from Winterbottom's book on Sierra Leone (published in 1803), it appeared as in the manuscript thesis.

He described himself on the title page as "James Africanus B. Horton," with his medical qualifications, army rank and membership in learned societies. The short preface was signed simply "Africanus Horton." In it he announced the forthcoming appearance of a larger work *On the Diseases of Tropical Climates,* "now in the press." But it was to be another eight years before his next medical work appeared and sixteen before he published *Diseases of Tropical Climates*—works that were to be based not on the superficial knowledge of a medical student, but on years of experience and observation in Africa.

III

RESEARCH, WAR, AND POLITICS

EARLY DIFFICULTIES

THE SIERRA LEONE COLONY lived up to its evil reputation in 1859. Epidemics of yellow fever, measles, and smallpox broke out, killing at least 500 in Freetown alone in a few months. Forty-two Europeans died—half the European population. The doctors fell ill too, leaving only one army surgeon to tend the sick. When Horton and Davies reached home in October they hoped to be allowed to stay for a while to look after their countrypeople. The leading citizens petitioned for them to stay. But with the end of the heavy rains the epidemics had ceased. The government felt there was no longer any urgent need for them, and to their disappointment they remained just one day and a half at home—just long enough for Horton to date the one-page preface of his *Medical Topography* from Freetown. Then they were sent down the coast to Ghana, for service in the garrisons of the British Gold Coast.[1]

The Danish government had sold its forts to the British in 1850. The Dutch still retained theirs. The British forts where Horton was stationed were garrisoned by the West India Regiments, soldiers recruited from the black population of the West Indies (with a few Africans) under white officers. Each regiment would serve alternately in the West Indies and in West Africa,

1. P.R.O., C.O. 267/264, Fitzjames, 176, Oct. 24, 1859; C.M.S., CAI/0117, Horton, Nov. 10, 1859.

moving regularly back and forth across the Atlantic.[2] The soldiers had just been put into romantic "Zouave" uniforms—tur-
bans, short jackets, and baggy trousers. The officers wore ordi-
nary military uniforms. Horton's, as a member of the Army Medical Department, was scarlet, faced with black velvet.

Round the forts clustered the seaside trading towns, dominated
by small merchant communities, the African and Eurafrican
"scholars," as those who had had a European-style education
were called, and a handful of Europeans. Like the Freetown
bourgeoisie, they lived with as much Europeanized elegance as
they could afford. A few immigrant Sierra Leoneans were settled
among them in trade or government service. Together they
formed a social community of their own. Horton therefore could
find congenial educated African companionship (as a change
from his white comrades in the officers' mess) in the coastal
towns where he was to spend much of the next twenty years.

He was posted to Anomabu, near Cape Coast, Davies to Dixcove, fifty miles to the east. During his early years of military
service Horton was moved continually from one station to another, living in one after another of the damp, tumbledown old
forts where the garrisons were quartered. When he died, the
author of his obituary in one of the Lagos newspapers suggested
that his military superiors had deliberately moved him about in
this way out of prejudice and malice, careless of the health and
comfort of a subordinate whose talents they resented.[3]

Certainly he contrasted strikingly with most of his brother
officers. The West Coast of Africa was one of the least sought
after British military stations. It was reputed to be frighteningly
unhealthy, and was of little interest to the British public. Expenditure was cut to a minimum: ambitious, energetic officers kept
away, for they knew they would have no chance of distinguishing
themselves. The West India Regiments had no social prestige.
Some officers only entered them to escape from creditors—even

2. Dr. Davidson Nicol has suggested in his *Africanus Horton,* p. 1, that Horton
might have crossed the Atlantic as medical officer in a troopship. There were
embarkations in 1861 and 1863 that he might have accompanied [see J. E.
Caulfeild, *A Hundred Years History of the 2nd Bttn West India Regiment*
(London, 1899), 125, 147], but I have no evidence that he did.
3. *Lagos Observer,* Nov. 8, 1883.

wives—in England. Idle and demoralized, with only perfunctory duties to perform, they had no incentive to take an interest in their work or in the country where they served.

No wonder then if they disliked the intrusion of an energetic outspoken African doctor into their somnolent officers' messes. Even a white officer who wrote serious books and took an active interest in everything going on around him would no doubt have excited their contempt and derision. The medical officers particularly resented having a black colleague, and saw in him a threat to their own status. Throughout his army career there were brother doctors ready to asperse him on one ground or another. But on one ground they could not asperse him—his professional skill. Even his bitter enemies never dared to allege that he was anything but an outstandingly capable and hard-working doctor.

Before leaving England he had been asked by the Director-General of the Army Medical Services, Thomas Alexander, for a report on his new station. He busied himself immediately, and within three weeks had sent off a dozen pages describing the town and geology of Anomabu, as well as the old fort where he was quartered. He included measurements of the rooms, and four drawings of the fort courtyard, concluding with a list of broken windows, roofs, and doors which let in the rain and made the place damp and unhealthy.[4]

Whatever interest his zeal may have excited in England, it left his immediate superiors unimpressed. The officer commanding the fort, Captain de Ruvignes, from the first day of his arrival persecuted and humiliated him in petty ways. "I did expect a degree of prejudice against us," Horton wrote later, "But not to such an extent." Not content with personal rudeness, de Ruvignes tried to undermine his authority with the soldiers, and to attack him indirectly through his servants, forbidding them to use the officers' kitchen (so that he would have to go without his dinner), and having one of them publicly flogged without a word of explanation.

4. Royal Army Medical Corps Historical Museum, Aldershot, Correspondence, 1859, Gold Coast (18835), Horton to Alexander, Nov. 7, 1859. I owe this reference to the kindness of Major General A. MacLennan.

An axiom of the European empires of race in Africa (and the British Empire during the nineteenth century grew steadily more race-conscious) was the belief that only a white man could command respect from non-white subordinates. The officers who wanted to be rid of Horton and Davies, unable to impugn their medical capabilities, declared that the soldiers under their command would not respect them. De Ruvignes tried to prove it, by encouraging the soldiers to slight Horton—but in vain. "On the contrary," Horton observed, *"I received the greatest respect from them."* It was hoped that these reiterated vexatious meannesses would provoke him into some act of violent retaliation for which he could be punished—perhaps even dismissed from the service altogether.

His friends urged him to complain to the commanding officer at Cape Coast, or write to his influential friends in England. But he remained calm. Before he and Davies left London, Henry Venn had told them, "Never to stand out too much for your rights—Be patient and time will bring it to you." Nor did Horton see his torments in a purely personal and selfish light. He subsequently wrote to Venn,

> It is a matter of paramount necessity that as I am amongst the first of the native Africans who have been educated by H.M. Government in the medical profession and sent out in the army as staff asst: Surgeon to practice that noble art amongst my own countrymen and those of the Europeans who may require our attendance, that I should not be too hasty in whatever I am about to undertake—not to give in to the dictates of passion, or to take rash measures which the nature of the trials which I was suffering merited. I felt that it was the keystone of the continuance of that noble plan of educating young Africans and sending them in (*sic*) the Coast. Should I give way thousands of those here who are hostile to the plan will have grounds to complain, they will use every means to dissuade you and the government from going on in that noble Cause which is fraught with blessings for Africa.[5]

He went on carrying out his duties punctiliously, and continuing his research, taking meteorological notes for use in his future writings. After three months his patience and self-control were rewarded. The acting-governor, Major Bird, got to hear

5. C.M.S., CAI/0117, Horton to Venn, Feb. 3, 1860.

what was going on, summoned him to Cape Coast, and then transferred him from Anomabu to Keta.

With great magnanimity he agreed not to bring charges against de Ruvignes, who was transferred to Accra, where he held the post of Civil Commandant. Shortly afterwards it was discovered that £1200 of public money that had passed through his hands was missing. Before the deficiency could be investigated, he resigned his post and hurried off surreptitiously to Gabon and eventually to England. There he remained on half pay until 1881, when he was allowed to retire from the army with the honorary rank of colonel.[6]

Only when Horton was settled in his new station (after having had all his baggage capsized from a canoe as he was landing through the surf) did he sit down and pour out his story in a letter to his "dear Father" Henry Venn at the C.M.S. A reply came back at once—but not from Venn. It was written by the Lay Secretary of the C.M.S., Major Hector Straith, a retired officer who had spent a profligate youth in the army in India, and then after a religious conversion devoted himself with great spiritual zeal to religious causes.[7] No word of sympathy was offered, only threats and preachings. Horton was warned that if he dared to complain the government might never again bring Africans to England for education. He was exhorted to be meek and humble:

> we still hope that instead of tracing your uncomfortable and unhappy position to those whose authority you must obey—and to whose defects you attribute your uneasiness; you will now look within and compare your proud spirit with that of Him who washed the feet of the disciples.[8]

Straith, indeed, was busy instructing him, self-righteously and censoriously, to do exactly what he had been doing already. Here spoke another missionary voice—the iron hand that Venn's kindly glove hid—determined to keep in lowly places those they were purporting to raise.

6. Correspondence in P.R.O., C.O. 96/62, 65, 66, 69; *Army Lists*.

7. E. Stock, *History of the Church Missionary Society* (London, 1899), vol. i, p. 372; vol. ii, p. 374.

8. C.M.S., CAI/L7 Straith to Horton, Feb. 18, 1860.

RESEARCH AT KETA

Horton only spent a few months at Keta, but used his time well. In the evenings he used to go out shooting on the marshy banks of the lagoon, or for walks along the Atlantic shore. All the time he was observing. Eventually he put his observations into a brief "Medical Topography of a part of the Awoonah Country" (in which Keta is situated). He followed his usual plan of describing the countryside (he added a map, drawn himself), and inferring from its characteristics the diseases likely to prevail, and how they might be prevented. He sent it to Dr. Alexander, who, however, died that year, ending a correspondence which had plainly stimulated Horton to intellectual activity (if, indeed, outside stimulus was ever necessary).[9]

Though this short piece was unsystematically arranged, it displayed a wide range of observation. He mentioned the various kinds of animals and fish (including a little drawing of a local fish-trap), detailing particularly the types of shell-fish he had found in the long shallow lagoon. He also listed a few plants, including a beautifully scented jasmine.

Keta was considered an unhealthy station, hot and malarious. Believing, with most contemporaries, that malaria was caused, as its name implied, by bad air, he assumed that at Keta it "arises from the banks of the lagoon which lies about three minutes' walk from the Fort." The old Danish fort where the garrison was quartered was falling to pieces. He recommended it be rebuilt, and suggested that the whole area could be made healthier by enforcing sanitary rules in the towns, and by planting trees, particularly coconut trees, along the banks of the lagoon: "the leaves, it would appear, have the power of decomposing malaria."

On his way from Keta to Accra, his next station, he made a detour to visit Lagos, still an independent kingdom in 1860. He was impressed by the growing city, a thriving commercial centre, with a cosmopolitan population. The year before the C.M.S.

9. Royal Army Medical Corps Historical Museum, Aldershot, Correspondence, 1859, Gold Coast (18835), "Medical Topography."

had opened Lagos Grammar School, under a principal of Yoruba descent, the Reverend T. B. Macaulay. Horton addressed the pupils, appearing—an African doctor in British officer's uniform—as a living example of what they too could hope to achieve. To stimulate them further he gave the principal fifty shillings as a prize for the best pupil.[10]

Next year Lagos was annexed as a British colony. Horton had no regrets. Deeply conscious of all that Britain had done for him, he looked forward with pleasure to all that he hoped it would do for Lagos. "We must unhesitatingly state," he wrote, "that it was the greatest blessing that could have happened to Lagos."[11]

Here he was voicing a view held by most Sierra Leone Creoles —that the British government should extend its responsibilities in West Africa. In Freetown public opinion regularly demanded that the frontiers be extended to take in the neighbouring peoples. Like him they tended to express their feelings in moral terms—as the introduction of civilization to backward peoples. But other motives intruded too. If British rule were extended, they would be the chief beneficiaries, enabled to use their own law and administration to make the country theirs. They saw themselves as pioneers carving out their own empire under the protection of the British flag, like their white compatriots in Australia, New Zealand, or the Canadian West.

Colonial governors, anxious to gain personal glory by annexations, often expressed sympathy with this view. But the British public remained uninterested. As we shall see, during Horton's lifetime there was to be little further expansion of British imperial responsibilities in West Africa.

"THIS MOST NOBLE UNDERTAKING"

From Accra Horton was posted almost at once back to Anomabu. By now the constant moving was wearing down his health. He had survived five British winters, but Africa was too much for

10. *Eagle and Lagos Critic*, Nov. 24, 1883.
11. James Africanus B. Horton, *West African Countries and Peoples*, 2nd ed. (Edinburgh, 1969), 143 (all page references are given to the second edition).

him. Though trained and appointed on the assumption that as an African he would be immune to tropical diseases, he nevertheless suffered from frequently recurring attacks of malaria. At Anomabu he was so ill that he had to go to headquarters at Cape Coast for medical treatment, which included "mercurial preparations with opium given internally." Sent out again, ostensibly cured, to Dixcove, he was again forced to return with severe dysentery. This time he was given three months' leave to go home to Freetown and recuperate.

During these two years of persecution, illness, and official duties he had found time to write, in addition to his report on Keta, a short treatise for the C.M.S., advising European missionaries how to preserve their health in the tropics,[12] a subject he was to return to later. But he was continually preoccupied with yet another theme—persuading the government to go on with the project he and Davies had inaugurated, the dream that had sustained him while he was being persecuted.

The War Office had been so pleased with Horton and Davies that they had asked the C.M.S. for half a dozen more candidates. Two were sent to London in 1857. One was rejected "as not being of the pure Negro race."[13] The other, George Manley, entered King's College and obtained a medical qualification. But he was considered to be mentally unbalanced and was sent home to Freetown. After this, the C.M.S. representatives in Sierra Leone sent no more candidates to England, and the plan lapsed.

Horton was determined that it should not be forgotten. In 1861 he sent the War Office a detailed reminder. He stressed particularly that African medical officers did not require annual leave, and therefore had time to study the country intensively, and carry on research. He pointed out what was never far from his mind, that the civilization of Africa

can never be properly accomplished unless by the aid of the educated *native portion of the community*. . . . It will, therefore, be of great importance to the country and to the people, should the Government continue to send to the Coast of Africa, *well educated natives,* sci-

12. In C.M.S., CAI/0117.
13. C.M.S., G/C. 1, vol. 32, minute of Dec. 11, 1857.

entific and professional men to serve in it, for the country will be largely benefitted by it.[14]

He and Davies, with their literary and mathematical education, had found it a strain having to keep up with the other students in London. He proposed that the government start a small medical training establishment in Freetown, run by an African instructor, where the young men chosen to study medicine could be grounded in anatomy, chemistry, and pharmacy. He added that they should also study the botany and natural history of West Africa, which they could not do abroad, to prepare them for research in their own country.

But the War Office was having second thoughts. At this period the British military forces in India were being reorganized. Officers were being appointed not, as until then, for service in India only, but for service anywhere. Several Indian doctors who had applied for army commissions were refused on the ground that they might have to serve in a cold climate for which they would be unsuited. This underhand way of introducing a colour bar into the service was questioned in Parliament. Government spokesmen reiterated their belief that Indians could not serve in northern climates without risk to themselves (though without explaining how it was that European doctors could safely serve in India).

However another, more honest, argument was produced—that the reorganized Army Medical Department now commanded a respect that it had never had before, and that it must be structured to retain the confidence of all ranks. By implication this meant a white army medical service. "We know," said Lord Herbert, "that Englishmen have not the same confidence in an Italian or a German doctor—to say nothing of an Indian doctor. . . ."[15]

This argument plainly excluded Africans. When, therefore, the Director-General of the Army Medical Department wrote asking the Principal Medical Officer in the Gold Coast, Dr. Charles O'Callaghan, for a report on Horton's proposal, he asked particu-

14. C.M.S., CAI/0117, contains copies of Horton's correspondence to the War Office.
15. *Parliamentary Debates* (new series), vol. clxi, pp. 794-96, 1643-65, 2098-2101; vol. clxiii, pp. 1391-1403; vol. clxiv, pp. 1381-87.

larly whether Horton and Davies "possess the confidence of the European and native community whom they may be called upon to treat."

Dr. O'Callaghan understood what he was being asked, and replied unequivocally that they did not "possess the confidence of the European community nor even the confidence of the native community in the Territory in the same degree as the European Medical Officers." In support of his view he explained, "The freemen of the tribes of this Protectorate are a proud and highbred race, and they regard the natives of Sierra Leone especially with a distrust and barbaric aversion of which but a feint (*sic*) conception can be entertained in England."

Here he was voicing the antagonism which Europeans were increasingly to express against educated Sierra Leoneans—expressing it indirectly, not imputing it to themselves, but to other Africans, and so laying the foundation for the future policy of divide and rule practised in British West Africa in the twentieth century.

The officer commanding the troops, Captain Brownwell, had been long in West Africa. Horton earlier had written of him that "he loves the Africans and is beloved by them." But he was easy-going and easily persuaded, not ready to oppose his medical colleague, and wrote to London supporting O'Callaghan. On the strength of these reports the War Office informed Horton that it did not propose to train any more African medical officers.

Horton would not abandon *"this most noble undertaking"* without a struggle. He collected from the governor and from the leading merchants evidence directly contradicting O'Callaghan's. Governor Richard Pine, who had served many years in West Africa, had been Horton's patient, and testified to the confidence he, and the members of the African community too, felt in him. The alleged "barbaric aversion" towards Sierra Leoneans was easily disposed of: Pine pointed out that several Creoles were successfully employed in government service in the Gold Coast and-had married there. S. C. Brew, a prominent Fanti trader at Anomabu, replied categorically, "I can only say that the person who advanced such a statement must know next to nothing of the Coast as such is diametrically opposed to the truth."

Horton forwarded their letters to the War Office, sending copies to the C.M.S. Committee in London, asking them to intercede.
But in vain. "Combined and warm opposition" to his project, as
he later put it, "nipped it in the bud."[16]

MARRIAGE

When Horton returned to Freetown in 1861, apart from the brief
visit in 1859, he had not been home for six years. (It may be that
his concern to have an African as head of his proposed medical
institution was an indirect way of getting himself back for a
while). During his convalescence there he established himself
as a member of the rising Creole elite by buying a house and by
marrying. For both house and wife he looked to members of his
own Ibo community.

He bought his house, in a good position in Wilberforce Street,
for £150 from an Ibo countryman, the Reverend Charles Knight.
Knight, who had been a schoolboy at Gloucester village some
fifteen years before Horton was born, had been ordained in 1848
as one of the first Methodist ministers in Sierra Leone. Three
years later Horton bought a second house, for £168, in a fashionable situation on the corner of Oxford and Rawdon Streets,
and leased it to the French consulate.[17] His being able to pay
such sums of money after only a few years' service, with an army
salary of only £182 a year, shows how successful he was as a private medical practitioner.

His wife was the daughter of a prominent Ibo recaptive, William Henry Pratt.[18] Pratt exemplified the aspirations and suc-
cesses of the new Freetown bourgeoisie. Liberated as a boy from
a slave ship, he had worked as a shop assistant until his European employer maliciously got him a two-year prison sentence
on a false charge of stealing. Not discouraged, once out of prison

16. Horton, *West African Countries,* 45.
17. Registrar-General's Office, Freetown, Conveyance Book, vol. 9, p. 212, conveyance dated April 10, 1862; Conveyance Book, vol. 13, p. 89, conveyance
dated May 11, 1865; Somerset House, London, Wills, vol. 627, no. 75 (1885),
Horton's will, paragraph 4.
18. Registrar-General's Office, Freetown, St George's Marriage Register, March
27, 1862.

he started as a trader, first in the streets, then in the import-export trade in which he prospered. Like most recaptives he was strongly attached to his church and to his own community—president of the Ibo association in Freetown, and of a committee to found Christian missions in the Ibo country. He had married the daughter of a retired army sergeant from Antigua (probably another Ibo descendant) who was settled in the Colony. She had previously lived with a senior white official, Benjamin Campbell, later British consul in Lagos: at that period such a liaison was a mark of social prestige.

Pratt was wealthy enough to send most of his eight children to Europe to be educated. Fannie Marietta, Horton's wife, had been to school in France and England. But one after another the eight died young. Horton included in his book *West African Countries and Peoples* a long tribute to one of his dead brothers-in-law, a gifted and promising young man. By 1875 all had died.

Fannie Horton was married less than three years. She died in 1865, aged only twenty-two, leaving a baby daughter, May Marietta, and lies buried beside her father, who had died a few months earlier, in the Pratt family vault in Circular Road Cemetery, Freetown.

Horton returned from Freetown to Cape Coast; as well as his medical duties he had charge of the supply department. Then he was sent off again to outstations. In August 1862 he was in Accra and witnessed a severe earthquake. From there he went as medical officer on a military expedition to the Krobo country. By April 1863 he was back at Anomabu again. A letter he wrote from there suggests that he was still under physical strain, for in one short letter he repeated two phrases twice over—"as you are aware is unknown is unknown," and a few lines later, "with as many plants with as many plants."[19]

In the fort at Anomabu a member of the prominent Bannerman family, the son of a Scottish father and an Ashanti mother, was serving a long prison sentence. A senior British official, with the connivance of Dr. O'Callaghan, had vindictively reduced his subsistence allowance in prison from 21 pence a day to 3. He

19. National Library of Scotland, Blackwoods MS 4181, fol. 312.

complained to London and Horton was asked to investigate. Horton sent in a strongly worded report to the governor about the virtually homicidal conditions under which Bannerman was being detained. In Sierra Leone at that time one could just about support life on threepence a day, but "in a country like this where a most exorbitant price is asked for the smallest article of food," it would scarcely buy seasoning for a meal, let alone a meal.[20] As Bannerman's health had suffered from this harsh treatment, he was eventually released.

Yet routine duties by no means filled his time. He was still regularly occupied with research, including geology, which had interested him since his student days. In his *Medical Topography* he had suggested a correlation between soil formation and human morbidity. He wrote later,

> The geological nature of the soil bears very important relations to the sanitary condition of a country—its configuration and geological character having a close connexion, within a certain limit, with certain pathological conditions of man.[21]

In 1862 he brought out a six-page pamphlet, *Geological Constitution of Ahanta, Gold Coast* (a study he was later to pursue in a more practical way). He had it published by M. H. Davies, a Freetown printer and newspaper proprietor (which makes it one of the few nineteenth-century publications to bear a Freetown imprint). In this short piece he faced the dilemma which confronted nineteenth-century Christians (and he remained all his life a sincere Christian) of reconciling the Bible account of creation with the discoveries made by geologists. He began his pamphlet,

> Prior to the Adamic epoch, when by Divine fiat this world was reconstituted and adapted for the existence of man and recent creation, important geological upheavals took place which led to the submergence of a large tract of land on the sea coast of Ahanta and Axim.

From there he went on to describe briefly the geography of the area, and the types of rock found there, particularly the gold-

20. P.R.O., C.O. 96/60, Pine 36, May 5, 1863.
21. Horton, *Physical and Medical Climate*, 106.

bearing rocks. He finished off with a summary of a contemporary argument over the origin of earthquakes (a topical theme in the Gold Coast in 1862), whether they were caused by chemical or by mechanical action, and concluded in favour of the latter.

He also went on with his botanical research—describing and making drawings of African plants. By 1863 he had described two hundred, and wrote to the Edinburgh publishing firm Blackwood suggesting he compile a *Botany of Africa* for them.[22] Nothing seems to have come of this project.

THE ANGLO–ASHANTI WAR OF 1863–64

During these years the export trade from the coastal ports was still small, and the market fluctuated greatly. A Ghanaian geographer has suggested that the real economic heart of the country was inland Kumasi, the Ashanti capital, where all the trade routes met, rather than the seaports.[23] Horton described the Ashanti as "the life blood of the Gold Coast commerce."

Many British officials found it hard to bear that Ashanti should flourish as an independent kingdom, unaffected by British influence. They resented it when the Asantahene (the king of Ashanti) addressed them as if he were the equal of their own queen. British propaganda always depicted Ashanti as a barbarous bloodstained despotism, which must one day be liberated and civilized. Horton, too, maintained that the Ashanti were "immersed in gross ignorance and superstition," but he admired their discipline and military organization. "They are a formidable enemy," he wrote, "and ought always to be much conciliated and tolerated."[24] Successive Asantahenes, for their part, were determined to maintain their sovereign rights and privileges, and above all to hold on to Dutch Elmina, for which they still remained landlords.

In 1862 an Ashanti discovered a lump of gold. Under Ashanti law all gold nuggets (as distinct from gold dust) belonged to the

22. National Library of Scotland, Blackwoods MS 4181, fol. 312.
23. Kwamina B. Dickson, *A Historical Geography of Ghana* (Cambridge, 1969), 214.
24. Horton, *West African Countries,* 110-11.

king—a regulation that was probably in origin anti-inflationary, to restrict the circulation of gold and maintain its value.[25] However he kept quiet about his discovery. When it was eventually found out and reported, he fled to the British protected area. The Asantahene, Kwaku Dua I, asked the British government to send him back as a fugitive criminal.

Governor Pine, who had been educated as a lawyer, refused to give up the fugitive, on the ground that no crime had yet been proved against him. The Asantahene sent a further request. Pine received the ambassador in the Palaver Hall at Cape Coast Castle, attended by his officials and military officers and many prominent Fanti. Horton, who subsequently described the scene, may have been among them.[26] Again Pine refused. This time the Asantahene, though, according to Horton, "one of the most peaceful rulers that has ever sat on the throne," felt himself to be unwarrantably insulted, and declared war. Horton, evaluating the situation later, while admitting that Pine was right according to the strict letter of the law, felt the king was fully justified in refusing to accept a decision that undermined his own sovereignty.

In March 1863, therefore, Ashanti troops crossed the Pra river, which the British regarded as the southern boundary of Ashanti, to punish their British and Fanti enemies. The British force that went out to meet them included regular soldiers (Horton among them), large Fanti contingents, and detachments raised by the African merchant families in the seaports. Once again, as in 1824, ignominy awaited British arms. The commander, Major Cochrane, having advanced towards the Ashanti, retreated again to the coast, leaving his Fanti allies to be slaughtered. The Ashanti then went round destroying Fanti towns and villages until the rainy season began. Then, having achieved their objective, avenging the insult to their sovereignty, they returned home again.

Pine meanwhile had gone to visit the troops. He fell seriously ill, and Horton had to bring him back to Cape Coast, never leav-

25. So it was in Ancient Ghana—see El-Bekri's description, quoted in translation in J. D. Fage, "Ancient Ghana," in *Transactions of the Historical Society of Ghana,* vol. iii, no. 2 (1957), 82.
26. Horton, *Letters,* 54-55.

ing him for two days and nights. "Your devoted attention," Pine wrote to him later, "judicious and watchful care under Providence, enabled me to live through the fatigues of my journey."[27]

Inevitably, Pine was determined to avenge this bitter humiliation of British pride. In London such far-off insults seemed less wounding. Nevertheless, the Secretary of State half-heartedly agreed to allow further military action. The West India Regiments were reinforced. A new commanding officer, Lieutenant-Colonel Conran, took over, and a British army again marched inland. Horton accompanied them, later recalling how the West Indian soldiers marched in high spirits through the thick humid forests, brilliant with exotic flowers and birds:

> . . . here and there were hideous reptiles of every shape, hue and kind, from the gigantic boa, performing amusing gyrations amongst the lofty trees around, down to the alligators, which basked leisurely in the sun.[28]

However, some soldiers fell ill. Horton was put in charge of them at a temporary base hospital, while the main body went on to the Pra. Weeks passed, and the rains began. The soldiers had built huts to live in, but had not thatched them properly; soon the floors were a mass of mud and water. Thick river fogs chilled them at night. Everything was soaked—indeed, they were almost under water. They fell sick and had to be cared for in makeshift hospitals, where they lay on the muddy ground in pools of rain. Conran returned to the coast ill; the senior medical officer followed; other medical officers died. Horton was left in charge. He wrote begging Conran to let them withdraw to the coast until the rains were over—but Pine had forbidden another humiliating withdrawal.[29]

Eventually the news reached London that soldiers were dying like flies in a remote jungle, in a war the British public had never heard of, against an enemy they had never even seen. The campaign was rapidly wound up and the troops recalled. With-

27. C.M.S., CAI/0117, Pine, Oct. 29, 1863, enclosed in Horton, Nov. 13, 1863.
28. Horton, *Letters*, 71.
29. *African Times*, July 23, 1864.

out firing a shot the Ashanti had again humbled their enemies. "The white men bring many cannon into the bush," said the Asantahene, "but the bush is stronger than the cannon."

The officials responsible for this disastrous campaign were chiefly concerned to justify themselves to their superiors in London.[30] Conran in his report to the War Office did commend a few of his officers, but nowhere mentioned Horton. Of Davies he merely recorded that he had been sent from the Pra camp to look after a detachment of soldiers in Denkyera.[31] The senior medical officer's report included only one reference to Horton and none to Davies. It noted that he had been given charge of the temporary base hospital: the reader would assume that he must have stayed there.[32] It nowhere indicated that he had been as far as the Pra—let alone that he had been left behind there in full medical command.

Indeed, far from receiving recognition for his labours, Horton seems to have suffered for them. For when the reinforcing troops were posted away, he was transferred, too—to the remotest station in British West Africa, the little garrison on MacCarthy's Island, 150 miles up the Gambia river.

SERVICE IN THE GAMBIA

The Gambia-Senegal country was convulsed during the mid-nineteenth century by one of the many Muslim *jihads* (holy wars) which followed successively in West Africa, beginning about 1725, and continuing into the era of the European partition. Basically these were wars in which strict Muslims tried to enforce their own practices on lax, syncretistic Muslims. Personal and political issues often obtruded too. In the Gambia the strict Muslims were called by Europeans "Marabouts," their opponents "Soninkes" (both misleading labels). Warfare raged fairly continuously round the little enclave of the coastal Gambia Colony and its remote outpost on MacCarthy's Island. Sometimes

30. P.R.O., C.O. 96/69 despatches by Pine, Hackett, Conran, Ross.
31. P.R.O., C.O. 96/66 War Office Aug. 19, 1864 enclosure; C.O. 96/69 War Office Feb. 13, 1865 enclosure.
32. Parliamentary Papers 1865, vol. xxxiii, pp. 329-35.

the Colony government was drawn in, usually on the "Soninke" side, as Europeans tended to mistrust and fear strict Muslims. Horton disliked them too, believing Islam to be a reactionary and repressive religion.

From time to time British territory was invaded and British subjects suffered. But neither party was primarily interested in attacking the Colony, from which they derived the benefits of trade and occasional mediation. Shortly before Horton arrived, war seemed to be threatening in the neighbourhood of MacCarthy's Island. The British commandant complained to the contestants, who agreed to move away and submit their future disputes to his arbitration.[33]

Horton therefore moved to a remote but peaceable station. The other inhabitants were chiefly Creole traders—a small community of about 600 people with their own Methodist church and school, looked after by a Creole pastor. Though peaceable it was not necessarily law-abiding. One day when Horton and his medical colleague were out, their quarters were robbed, and he lost his gold watch and about £150 worth of African gold jewellry.[34]

He seems not to have stayed continuously in the Gambia. In January 1866 he visited Monrovia, the capital of the Republic of Liberia. Founded in 1822 by the American Colonization Society as a home for immigrants of African descent from the United States, Liberia, like the Sierra Leone Colony, had suffered the early difficulties of any pioneer settlement. It then settled down to a period of short-lived prosperity (though always at a low economic level), which by 1866 was drawing to an end. Horton was pleased to see the Liberians carrying on their government competently, and looked forward to their occupying "an important place in regenerated Africa." But he was critical of what he saw, too—the squalid, neglected appearance of Monrovia harbour, and the lack of interest in educating the indigenous population.[35]

On this visit he presumably met the distinguished Liberian

33. J. A. Gray, *A History of the Gambia* (London, 1939), 424-25.
34. *African Times,* Jan. 23, 1866.
35. Horton, *West African Countries,* 16, 243-44.

scholar Edward Blyden, who was in Monrovia at that date.[36] Horton referred to him later as "my friend," and thought highly of him. Blyden's background was very different from his. Born three years earlier than Horton, of African descent in the Danish West Indies, Blyden had been refused a university education in the United States because of his colour. He then emigrated to Liberia. Hence he had known from youth the racial prejudice that Horton was spared until adulthood, and was to evolve a very different theory of race.

An international Industrial Exhibition was held in Freetown in 1865. Almost the only items of any scientific interest among the meagre Sierra Leone exhibits were supplied by Horton. As well as samples of Mandinka and Wolof leatherwork and metalwork from the Gambia, he sent botanical and medical specimens, including a preserved guinea worm, a parasite he was later to write a book about, and rock samples from his geological collection.[37]

But, influenced no doubt by the cruel rebuff from the War Office, he now turned increasingly to politics. Here, as a serving officer, he was always vulnerable. His enemies could allege that his political activities were evidence of disloyalty and insubordination. Somehow he had to steer a course that would enable him to criticize the government constructively, without swerving from the military duty of supporting it loyally.

RACE AND POLITICS

The African Aid Society was founded in London in 1860, one of many successive organizations devoted to the combined aim of advancing business and philanthropy in Africa. Its sponsors took up the policies proposed twenty years earlier by Sir T. F. Buxton —the suppression of slave trade and slavery, and African economic development. This attracted Horton, who wanted to develop his country's wealth for its peoples' benefit. Like most such

36. Edith Holden, *Blyden of Liberia* (New York, 1966), chapter x; for Blyden's career and place in history see Hollis R. Lynch, *Edward Wilmot Blyden* (London, 1967).
37. *Industrial Exhibition at Sierra Leone* (London, 1866).

organizations it was sponsored by influential men. The chairman was Lord Alfred Churchill, who sat on various philanthropic committees. Among them was the Institut d'Afrique in Paris, of which he was a vice-president. Horton later became a member of this body—perhaps through Churchill's recommendation.

The society published its own monthly newspaper in London, the *African Times*. It quickly became a mouthpiece for educated Africans. Complaints against officials, hitherto only publicized, if at all, in local newspapers, were given an airing through its pages up and down the coast and in England. General political issues too were raised, such as the need to expand the frontiers of the coastal colonies inland, or the lack of political representation.

The editor, Ferdinand Fitzgerald, was something of an eccentric—a militant and violently evangelical Irish Protestant who believed the earth was flat. He dedicated himself uncompromisingly and self-righteously to the cause of African advancement and development Usually uncritical in his championship, he was sometimes deluded into taking up worthless causes. But most of the grievances he raised were genuine, and would otherwise have remained hidden behind the veil of official secrecy that deliberately concealed policy in the British West African colonies. He was not afraid of publicizing in print the kind of criticisms that were normally only uttered privately: he commented, for instance, on Horton's relegation to MacCarthy's Island after his services in the Ashanti campaign.[38] Nor was he deterred by fear of legal proceedings from printing actionable statements about alleged evil-doers.

His language tended to be excitable, whether he was denouncing the errors of the Pope or the misdeeds of a colonial governor. The respectable African Aid Society took fright and gave up the *African Times* in 1866. But he continued it as a venture of his own, publishing it in connexion with an import-export agency. His public utterances were reinforced by regular letters of advice and complaint to the Colonial Office, where the officials regarded him as a poisonous trouble-maker.

Horton saw in the *African Times* a means of circulating his

38. *African Times,* Aug. 23, 1864.

own views to the literate West African public. He helped Fitzgerald collect subscriptions, and even raised £24 from the inhabitants of MacCarthy's Island as a donation to the African Aid
Society. The society recommended to the War Office his plan for
training more African doctors, and publicized it in the *African
Times*. He published letters in its pages on the need to develop
African agriculture, and a plan to build a sanatorium on the
mountains above Freetown, as well as occasional anonymous
contributions.[39] But a series of letters published in 1866 and 1868
signed "Sunacirfa" ("Africanus" backwards) seems not to have
been written by him but by someone resident in Freetown.

   In 1864 Fitzgerald wrote asking him "what in the opinion of
an African are the chief political wants of this Coast?"[40] The
question was not merely an expression of polite curiosity. The
news of the Anglo–Ashanti War of 1863–64 had outraged many
people in Britain. Lives had been lost and large sums of their
money spent for objectives they cared nothing about. Latent
prejudice against West Africa was always easy to rouse.

   In any case colonies were unpopular in mid-nineteenth century
Britain. They offered no obvious economic advantages in a free
trade era, when British manufactures sold as easily outside the
empire as inside. The Canadian, Australian, and New Zealand colonies seemed to be preparing to follow the former American
colonies into independence. Indeed, it was widely asserted that colonies brought more trouble and expense than advantage and
should be abandoned altogether.

   Those who wanted arguments against West Africa could draw
them from the increasingly prevalent theories of race. In 1850
Robert Knox, an Edinburgh doctor who had once served (like
Horton) as an army doctor in Africa, published his *Races of Men,*
based on public lectures he had been giving over the previous
decade. In France his better-known contemporary, Arthur de
Gobineau, published his *Essai sur l'Inégalité des Races Humaines*
in 1853. Both interpreted the movements of history and society

---

39. Ibid. May 23, 1864, Jan. 23, 1865, June 23, 1863; Horton, *Letters,* 55.
40. James Africanus B. Horton, *Political Economy of British Western Africa*
(London, 1865), v.

in racial terms. In Knox's words, "Race is everything," in Gobineau's, "race holds the key," to the understanding of all human activity.[41] Both saw as the underlying force in society the struggle not of classes nor of nations but of races.

Both believed that all human beings are imprisoned in irrevocable categories of race. They believed the distinctions between races to be psychological as well as physical—for if they were only physical they would be unimportant. This implied that human behaviour, as well as appearance, could be predicted by racial classification. They assumed that innate hostility between the races kept them permanently apart, and that races could be arranged hierarchically, white at the top, black at the bottom.

Neither Knox's nor Gobineau's books have ever had a wide readership. Yet the theory they expounded became widely popular in Europe and white America. Scientists took it seriously. The Anthropological Society of London was founded in 1863 to collect evidence to test (in practice, to substantiate) the racial hypothesis. Captain (later Sir) Richard Burton, whom Horton once described as "the most determined African hater," was a vice-president.

Burton had a grudge against society. Forced out of the British army in India, he had travelled extensively over southwest Asia and East Africa, reaching many places until then unknown to Europeans. The British Foreign Office sent him as consul to the Bight of Benin. On his way down the coast in 1861 he stopped at the various settlements, a day or two in each, and then published his impressions in a long-winded, superficial travel book, *Wanderings in West Africa*.

He did not mention Horton in his book, but praised Horton's persecutor, de Ruvignes, whom he met in Accra and revisited him there in July 1862.[42] Horton was in Accra in August, so conceivably they might have met. But neither mentioned a meeting in any of their published works.

Convinced that whites were innately superior to blacks ("I do

41. Robert Knox, *Races of Men* (London, 1850), 2; Arthur de Gobineau, *Essai sur l'Inégalité des Races Humaines* (Paris, 1853), vi.
42. R. F. Burton and V. L. Cameron, *To the Gold Coast for Gold* (London, 1883), vol. ii, p. 348n.

not hold the black to be equal to the white," he once informed the Foreign Office[43]), Burton resented any attempt to disprove it. Hence he hated educated Africans viciously and unforgivingly. An undercurrent of contempt and aversion runs through the book: no chance is missed to sneer at them. It is true that, as Horton was later to point out, Burton was not always consistent. He observed that the Africans on the Gold Coast seemed to be superior to the Europeans resident there. But this was merely meant as a slur on the Gold Coast Europeans. Burton was always ready to savage anyone, black or white. On the Creoles he had only evil to report, lashing out viciously in a style, to quote Horton, "personally abusive, turgidly illustrative, and illogically argumentative."

With hatred of educated Africans went hatred of the Christian missionaries who had given them a chance to rise in the world. He could only sneer at the kind of schools where Horton had been educated. In any case he disliked Christianity. During his travels he had become fascinated by Islam. As Muslims were not interested in advancing themselves socially to equality with Europeans, he could accept them with patronizing praise. They did not compete with the white man. His anti-missionary views won him popularity in England with those who were bored with the humanitarian tradition—the tradition Charles Dickens satirized in *Bleak House,* where Mrs. Jellaby neglects her children and devotes her time to saving the souls of far-off Africans.

Wanderings in West Africa, concocted though it was out of trivial gossip and prejudiced, superficial observation, by a stranger to the country, was nevertheless extremely influential. Its anecdotes and assertions were a rich quarry for racists. Burton's fame as a traveller gave authority to what he wrote. Stay-at-homes felt they must believe him. "Probably there is no Englishman or indeed European living," a Colonial Office official minuted in 1862 on a report by Burton, "who is as well qualified as the writer to give an opinion in a question of African character and conduct. He is the celebrated traveller and linguist. . . ."[44]

43. P.R.O., F.O. 97/438, Burton, June 5, 1867.
44. P.R.O., C.O. 147/2, minute by Elliot, F. O., Jan. 15, 1862.

Burton's name, then, conferred prestige on the Anthropological Society. Most of its publications were written from the standpoint he adopted—that black was inferior to white. Dr. James Hunt, the president of the Society, spelt this out in 1863 in a published presidential address on "The Negro's Place in Nature."[45] Horton perceptively called it a "pro-slavery paper." For the arguments brought up by English racists in London could just as well be used to uphold the champions of slavery in the United States who were at that moment fighting for the right to cling on to their human property.[46]

Swayed by arguments of politics, economics, emotion, and race, Parliament appointed a committee in 1865 to consider whether the West African colonies were worth keeping. The witnesses who gave evidence were chiefly European officials, missionaries, and traders. Only one African gave evidence—the representative of King Aggrey of Cape Coast. Neither Horton, nor Davies, nor Bishop Crowther, nor any of the Gold Coast African merchants were heard. Burton, however, was given a long hearing, and was encouraged by the chairman to air his malicious propensities.

Most of the traders who gave evidence felt that the colonies brought them little advantage. They preferred to trade beyond British jurisdiction, in places where there were no officials to interfere with them. A few missionaries too were prepared to welcome a British withdrawal. The officials, however, were obviously not going to recommend the abolition of their own jobs. The committee had to compromise.

They recommended, largely for reasons of economy, that the four colonies be united under one governor-in-chief resident in Freetown. Immediate withdrawal was recommended only from MacCarthy's Island. Further annexations in West Africa were advised against but not absolutely forbidden. Ultimate withdrawal from all the colonies, except probably Sierra Leone with its valuable harbour, was envisaged for the future. These recommendations were adopted as resolutions of the House of Commons.

45. Published separately, and in *Memoirs of the Anthropological Society of London, 1863-64* (London, 1865).
46. *African Times*, Apr. 23, 1866.

In practice they scarcely altered British policy. A government that wanted to contract responsibilities could invoke them; a government that wanted to extend responsibilities could ignore them. In fact, not even MacCarthy's Island was to be abandoned. But this the public could not know. The resolutions declared that British policy-makers were not interested in West Africa, and those who read them were justified in assuming that they meant what they said.

The French government, for instance, immediately established protectorates over the coastline north of Sierra Leone, correctly assuming that the British government would make no objection. The resolutions also alerted educated Africans. For at the suggestion of the Secretary of State, Edward Cardwell, they contained the words,

> . . . the object of our policy should be to encourage in the natives the exercise of those qualities which may render it possible more and more to transfer to them the administration of the governments. . . .[47]

Here was an explicit promise to the African citizens of British West Africa that they, like the Canadians and Australians, were to move towards eventual self-government.

Nor was this any great surprise to some of them. The Sierra Leone Creoles, as British subjects, were entitled to believe that they inherited an Englishman's right to be ruled by a government of his own choosing. The 1865 resolutions appeared to confirm this right: they seemed a charter of liberties. Horton certainly interpreted them in this way. From now on he was inspired by the vision of a West Africa freed from colonial rule, and was to concern himself with the practical details "of establishing independent African nationalities."

He took Fitzgerald's request for an African's opinion on the requirements of West Africa as a starting point, and sketched out his views in a 36-page pamphlet, *Political Economy of British West Africa*. It was presented in the form of an address to the African Aid Society, and published by the printer of the *African Times*, dated from Bathurst, River Gambia, August 1865. In it

47. Parliamentary Papers 1865, vol. v, p. xvi.

he sketched out the themes he was later to develop fully in *West African Countries and Peoples*.[48]

The first half was a theoretical statement of African capabilities, witnessed particularly by the achievements of his own Sierra Leone compatriots. He answered Hunt's condemnations—indeed, the pamphlet is subtitled *The African's View of the Negro's Place in Nature*, deliberately echoing the title of Hunt's lecture. Here, and in a review of the lecture published later in the *African Times*, Horton convicted him of ignorance and prejudice. Hunt's ignorance was displayed by the second-hand, inaccurate evidence he used to make his case. His prejudice he displayed by his choice of authorities, including Burton, and his readiness "to select the worst possible specimens, and make them typical of the whole African race," but to display as the typical European "the most perfect and model form." This, he rightly observed, has always been the practice of white racists.[49]

In the second half of the pamphlet he explained what he saw as the requirements of the four colonies, ranging widely, but briefly, over constitutional, educational, fiscal, agricultural, and sanitary reforms. He added a prefatory note deploring recent trends in Sierra Leone where he heard that the European community—stimulated by Burton and encouraged, he believed, by the governor—was displaying an unwonted colour hostility against the Creole population.

Sketchy and hastily written though his pamphlet was, it showed interested people in Britain that there were thoughtful educated Africans in the British colonies ready to respond to the 1865 committee's proposal to encourage the development of self-government.

SELF-GOVERNMENT ON MacCARTHY'S ISLAND

Horton was now fortuitously presented with a chance to mount a small-scale rehearsal for eventual self-government. The Parliamentary committee had recommended that MacCarthy's Island,

48. In *West African Countries* he refers to *Political Economy* as "the first edition of this work" (p. 230).
49. *African Times,* Apr. 23, 1866.

where he was stationed, should be given up. Just at the moment when the troops were being ordered to withdraw, a Soninke king raided the neighbouring country, alarming the islanders. A party of troops, with Horton as medical officer, went out to ward off invasion (if, indeed, any had been intended), and the raiders withdrew.[50] The islanders, who had been joined by refugees from the surrounding wars, now complained that if the government abandoned them they would be left at the mercy of their aggressive neighbours. The military authorities in London refused to change their minds, but the government in Bathurst agreed to send a magistrate and a few police constables to give the island at least nominal protection.

When the detachment of soldiers withdrew in June 1866, Horton stayed behind as commandant until the magistrate arrived from Bathurst. He summoned the leading inhabitants and invited them to form a provisional government. They agreed to recruit and pay a dozen volunteer constables, and were themselves sworn in as special constables. A few simple public safety rules were agreed to. For a few days they maintained a self-governing community. When the magistrate arrived, they disbanded themselves, paying the balance of the money subscribed for constables to the Creole minister on the island to repair his church. "This," Horton commented, "is an excellent manifestation of a spirit of self-government."[51]

He then returned to Bathurst where a yellow fever epidemic raged from June to August: two European medical officers were among the victims.[52] In January he was transferred back to Cape Coast and posted to Accra. He liked Accra—"the picnic spot of Western Africa," he called it—with its cosmopolitan population and relaxed ways. "In no part of the Coast is the caste distinction of colour so trampled under foot as at this place."[53] Here he could enjoy a social life very different from the snobbish, official-

---

50. P.R.O., C.O. 87/84, D'Arcy, 175, Apr. 23, 1866; *Hart's Army List,* 1873, 393.
51. *African Times,* July 23, 1866; Horton, *West African Countries,* 77-79.
52. Horton, *Physical and Medical Climate,* 238; Governor D'Arcy, however, stated in a despatch that the European military medical officer, Dr Mosse, was there single-handed (P.R.O., C.O. 87/84, D'Arcy Sept. 23, 1866).
53. Horton, *West African Countries,* 124-25.

ridden life of Cape Coast, with its petty hierarchical distinctions. As well as his routine duties, he acted as a magistrate, and went out as medical officer with a detachment of soldiers on an expedition to Ada—where of course he found time for geological research.[54]

In September he was granted leave to go to England. He stayed there nearly a year, and published three books. Two were medical—*Physical and Medical Climate and Meteorology of the West Coast of Africa,* and *Guinea Worm, or Dracunculus.* The third was the revision of his *Political Economy,* entitled *West African Countries and Peoples.*

.

54. *African Times,* Apr.–Sept., 1867.

IV

WEST AFRICAN COUNTRIES
AND PEOPLES

WEST AFRICAN COUNTRIES AND PEOPLES—RACE

HORTON BROUGHT the incomplete manuscript of *West African Countries and Peoples* to England and finished it there. The preface is dated December 1867. A few footnotes were added while the book was with the printer and it was advertised as ready in the *African Times* for June 1868. Most of it must have been written in West Africa during the intervals from his medical, military, and magisterial duties, while he was constantly being moved about from one station to another—and simultaneously working on his medical books. Written in such a way, and finished off in haste, it lacks polish, and contains some inconsistencies that further revision would no doubt have removed.

The book displayed a wide range of reading, supported by apposite quotations. Some, no doubt, were remembered from his schooldays—lines from the Greek and Latin classics, from Bacon's essays and Niebuhr's *History of Rome*—the diet he will have been fed on at the Grammar School and Fourah Bay College. Others were from contemporary political writers like Herman Merivale and Lord Holland. He made use of the principal published descriptions of West Africa—the successive Parliamentary reports, and recent books by Baikie, Du Chaillu, Bishop Crowther, and even Burton. For though he ridiculed and controverted Burton's outpourings on race, he was ready to learn from his factual descriptions of places he had not visited himself, such as Abeokuta or East Africa.

Another source he used was Wilson Armistead's vast compilation *A Tribute for the Negro*, published in 1848. But to write, as David Kimble has done,[1] that "some of the very phrases" he used "were probably taken direct" from Armistead implies wholesale plagiarism. This he was not guilty of. He acknowledged his occasional borrowings from Armistead quite openly (there is no "probably" about it), and from the other authors whose work he used.

He was also familiar with the principal writings on race—on his own side Prichard and Quatrefages, against him Knox, Hunt, Pruner Bey, and Carl Vogt. Plainly, when he moved about from one fort to another, or to the Gambia and back, he must have carried a substantial library with him. Such hazards as the capsizing of his baggage into the sea at Keta in 1860 must have exposed him to great potential loss.

It was published in London by W. J. Johnson who printed the *African Times* and had already published his *Political Economy*. Horton paid for publication himself. In 1870 he stated, "it has cost me about two hundred and fifty pounds for publishing works on Western Africa." He went on to comment that "works on Western Africa, unless written to attract the fancy or to excite wonder, by recording acts of heroic enterprise, like the gorilla hunting etc., are a dead loss to the writer."[2] He prefixed a long dedication to Henry Venn. On the title page is a remark made in 1818 by the Emperor Alexander I of Russia to Thomas Clarkson, "Africa ought to be allowed to have a fair chance of raising her character in the scale of the civilized world"—a summary of Horton's own underlying theme.

His qualifications on the title page now included Fellow of the Royal Geographical Society, which he had joined in 1868. As before, he appeared as "James Africanus B. Horton," and at the end of the preface as "Africanus Horton"—and to make his African identity unequivocal he bracketed "Native of Sierra Leone." A map of the western half of Africa was included, per-

1. David Kimble, *A Political History of Ghana* (London, 1963), 538n.
2. Horton, *Letters,* viii.

haps because a reviewer had deplored the lack of a map in his already published *Physical and Medical Climate*.[3] But though it bears his name he did not draw it. It was produced by the London cartographic firm of James Wyld—and had already appeared five years earlier to illustrate Burton's *Wanderings in West Africa*.

His objectives were formulated in a lengthy book-title, *West African Countries and Peoples, British and Native. With the Requirements necessary for establishing that self government recommended by the Committee of the House of Commons, 1865; and a Vindication of the African Race*. They were practical, pragmatic objectives, typical of this practical, pragmatic officer. He provided an ignorant British public with useful information about West Africa. He outlined a programme for its evolution towards self government. And he gave his own view of, to quote James Hunt's title, "The Negro's place in Nature."

Hunt had recently published in translation a series of lectures by Carl Vogt, a German scholar who taught at the University of Geneva. These lectures upheld his own belief that mankind is imprisoned in unalterable categories of race, that racial characteristics are moral as well as physical, and that the dark races are irrevocably inferior to the light.[4] In answering him Horton was not merely concerned with a theoretical vindication of African capabilities. He realized that if such theories were generally adopted, there would be no hope of carrying out the 1865 resolutions. For no one would be interested in the advancement of Africans if they believed that Africans were incapable of advancing.

He had already seen how some members of the 1865 committee had adopted Burton's views, and how "leading statesmen of the present day have showed themselves easily carried away by the malicious views of these negrophobists." His arguments about race were therefore an essential part of his political blueprint for West Africa.

The racial theorists were unable to define "race" precisely.

3. *The Lancet*, Feb. 1, 1868, p. 164.
4. Carl Vogt, *Lectures on Man*, ed. by J. Hunt (London, 1864).

Knox admitted that his "Races of Men" were classified in an arbitrary way. So did Gobineau. Horton used the term as they did, to indicate the implied hereditary component in any group of people. He applied it indiscriminately in varying contexts. Sometimes he used it as an apparently physical label, as in "negro race,"[5] sometimes as a geographical label, as in "African" or "European" race, sometimes political, as when he called the Temne, Serer, Ashanti, or English "races," and sometimes cultural or religious. He called the Gambia "Marabouts" a race, though their bond of identity was not one of descent, but their strict attachment to Islam.

What in his opponents was a weakness, an inability to isolate their basic concept, was in him a strength, since he did not regard racial characteristics as fixed and unalterable. He believed that the variations between human groups depended on nurture and environment, and that any "race" could be improved by education, and degraded by the lack of it. Here he followed James Cowles Prichard, an Edinburgh graduate of a previous generation, whose evolutionary theories of race looked forward to Darwin.[6] Horton did not quote Darwin's *Origin of Species*: perhaps it had not yet reached him in West Africa. For although Darwin's theories were used with fixed race implications by "Social Darwinists," strictly they are incompatible with fixed race theory and confirm Horton's contention that race is an alterable category in human beings.

Like most of his European contemporaries, he saw human history as a progress from barbarism to civilization, and assumed that nineteenth-century Europe represented the highest form of civilization yet attained. But he did not go on to deduce that Europeans were therefore innately and permanently superior. He recalled how the peoples of Europe had themselves emerged from barbarism—how the Romans had despised the Ancient Britons, and how the Greeks and Romans had venerated Africa as the fount of wisdom. West Africans, he maintained, were now emerg-

5. "Negro" appeared in *West African Countries* with a lower case initial.
6. For Prichard see Michael Banton, "Race as a Social Category," in *Race,* vol. viii, 1 (1966); for Prichard's influence on Horton see George Shepperson's introduction to the second edition of *West African Countries,* xx.

ing from barbarism, like the Britons long ago and the Russians more recently, and were proving as capable of being civilized as the peoples of Europe.[7]

As evidence of African capability he instanced his own Creole people, now "blending into one race," who after only one generation of missionary instruction were spreading all over West Africa as the pioneers of civilization, "an industrious exploring race," like their English mentors.[8]

> Fancy a lot of slaves—unlettered, rude, naked, possessing no knowledge of the useful arts—thrown into a wild country, to cut down the woods and build towns; fancy these ragged wild natives under British, and, consequently, civilized influences, after a lapse of a few years becoming large landowners, possessing large mercantile establishments and money, claiming a voice in the legislative government, and giving their offspring proper English and foreign education; and dare you tell me that the African is not susceptible of improvement of the highest order, that he does not possess in himself a principle of progression and a desire of perfection far surpassing many existing nations—since it cannot be shown in the world's history that any people with so limited advantages has shown such results within fifty years.[9]

With such empirical arguments Horton had no difficulty in controverting his opponents' theories. Whether or not they wrote (as they purported to) in a spirit of objective inquiry, they had produced inadequate data to validate them. He only needed to quote a few passages from Carl Vogt's "exuberant, ignorant eloquence" to reveal that Vogt knew nothing of Africa or of Africans. Burton, who did know Africa, he convicted of inconsistency and prejudice. The much-cited racial investigations of Pruner Bey, physician to the Khedive of Egypt, he showed to have been based on a few untypical physical specimens. He concluded that before scientists began pontificating about Africans, they must learn more about them—and reiterated his plea to the War Office for the establishment of a medical school in West Africa to sponsor research.[10]

7. Horton, *West African Countries*, 58-60.
8. Ibid., 83, 55-56.
9. Ibid. 24.
10. Ibid. 31-52.

In answering his opponents' racial theories empirically he laid himself open to possible empirical arguments against his own. As evidence for his belief that racial characteristics depend on environment, he stated that European children in the tropics, if not very carefully brought up, will "become exceedingly dark, and show a marked difference in their form, proportion and features."[11] Like Knox, Gobineau, and his friend Edward Blyden, he believed (though, like them, he brought no evidence to prove) that Europeans could not sustain themselves permanently in Africa—that if not renewed by white immigration or by marriage with Africans, they must die out "in about two generations." This widespread belief was shared by the 1865 committee, which declared that "the English race can never colonize West Africa."[12]

He was also inconsistent over mulattos. Mulattos were an obstacle to those who believed in a theory of fixed race—indeed, their very existence contradicted it. Hence racial theorists argued warily about "hybridity." Knox and Gobineau both held that a mulatto population could not sustain itself, and must die out if not revived by mixture from a pure stock. Vogt, admitting that all the evidence seemed to point against their theory, was still inclined to believe that it might somehow be true. Burton told the 1865 committee that it was still a matter of doubt whether mulattos could breed: he had no doubt, though, that whether or not they were sterile, they were vicious and immoral.

Horton defended them against this sweeping attack. If some were vicious, others, he declared, "adorn and enliven society"; he was to marry one himself a few years later. He praised the Swiss Basel missionaries for their readiness to marry Africans, and commented that the children of Temne mothers and European fathers were "intelligent and hard-working."[13] But elsewhere in the book he seemed to suggest the contrary, instancing the Nova Scotians in Freetown and the Wolof in the Gambia as communities that had degenerated through marriage with Europeans. And when he wrote on Liberia he declared that a "purely mulatto population cannot exist for any lengthened period; they

11. Ibid. 43-44.
12. Ibid. 68, 96.
13. Ibid. 49, 131, 86.

must either merge into one or other races (black or white), or gradually die out."[14]

Here he seems to have been reproducing unreflectingly the opinions of Edward Blyden, from whom he drew much of his information on Liberia, but without thinking through their implications. He was writing in a hurry and inevitably was led into inconsistencies in this hastily produced book. For Blyden's theory of race differed fundamentally from his own.[15] Blyden believed, with the white racists, that races were fixed and must not be mixed. Where he disagreed with them was in apportioning good attributes, and not just bad, to the non-white races. This belief in racial immutability, irreconcilable with Horton's theory of race, was shared, and even given an implied divine sanction, by Horton's Creole compatriot, James Johnson, in the words, "God does not intend to have the races confounded."[16]

The "Vindication" chapters end with a quotation from the Scottish philosopher Dugald Stewart, on the cyclical mutations of human society, and the rise and decline of successive peoples, doomed "to run alternately the career of improvement and of degeneracy." Horton commented,

> Such being the tendency of all national greatness, the nations of Western Africa must live in the hope, that in process of time their turn will come. . . .[17]

But he was no quietistic philosopher asking Africans to sit patiently awaiting the turn of fortune's wheel. He demanded from them the hard work and inventiveness which had activated the peoples of Europe—and had always activated him. In his final chapter he quoted a warning which the Liberian poet Hilary Teage had addressed to his countrymen,

> You are to give the answer whether the African race is doomed to interminable degradation—a hideous blot on the fair face of creation, a libel upon the dignity of human nature; or whether they are

14. Ibid. 26, 69-70, 244.
15. For Blyden's racial theories see Hollis R. Lynch, *Edward Wilmot Blyden: Pan-Negro Patriot 1832–1912* (London, 1967).
16. Quoted in E. A. Ayandele, *Holy Johnson* (London, 1970), 285.
17. Horton, *West African Countries*, 60-61.

capable to take an honourable rank amongst the great family of nations.[18]

The rest of the book is intended to guide the West African peoples into their honourable rank.

WEST AFRICAN COUNTRIES AND PEOPLES—POLITICS

The first chapter is headed "Description of the Original and Uncivilized State of the Native Tribes." Yet, though he used the word "tribes," he made it immediately clear that he was writing about "nations," and that each community had

> as truly a political Government as that of France or England. . . . Examining Western Africa in its entirety, we find it to be composed of a number of political communities, each ruled by a national Government.[19]

He did not therefore see Africa as a *tabula rasa*, to be shaped according to his own dreams, but as a continent already divided up into organized, though still undeveloped, nations, which ought to develop according to the example set by the more sophisticated nations of Europe.

He felt they had a long way to go. Like the European travellers whose works he quoted, he depicted most African institutions and customs as barbarous. Everything that seemed to hold them back from development he rejected, even if it was in itself justifiable. Domestic slavery, he admitted, was often humane and kindly, but he insisted that it must be abolished, because it made people lazy and unenterprising. He despised African religions, because he felt that they kept their devotees back in ignorance and subservience, while the Protestant Christianity he had been bred in, encouraged hard work and enterprise. Nor did he think much better of Islam. He condemned whole-heartedly Burton's contention that it was the most suitable religion for Africa.

> I believe and firmly hold, that it is not by Mohammedanizing the inhabitants of Western Africa according to the present school of anthropologists, that they can or will be civilized. . . . The people had

18. Ibid. 246.
19. Ibid. 4.

far better remain as they are, than to have any other religious belief except the Christian introduced and propagated amongst them.[20]

Those who have grown up in an intellectual climate of cultural relativism may feel embarrassed by Horton's uncompromising preference for European culture. But it followed consistently from his upbringing. His own Creole people had risen in the world by adopting the opportunities Europe offered, and rejected those elements in their African past that conflicted with them. He hoped to see all the West African nations following their example. But he was not asking them to give up their own African identity. When Africa's turn came, it would no more be a copy of Europe than the British Empire was a copy of the Roman Empire: "no Government can be copied from a plan." Whatever Africa learnt from Europe would have to be assimilated, in order to incorporate "the African element, so essential to African civilization."

As a contrast to the still "uncivilized" nations, he inserted a short piece on Liberia, as an example of a progressive African state. In 1868 this was still possible. Six years earlier Charles Dickens, normally contemptuous of humanitarian projects in Africa, had applauded Liberia as "the triumphant instance of the educability and power of self-government, and political capacity of the Negro."[21] Even Burton called the Liberians civilized.[22] But had Horton written three years later, in 1871, when the Republic had become ensnared by foreign debt, and was being torn apart by its only political revolution, he could not have painted such an encouraging picture.

Most of the book is occupied by his main theme—the development of "African nationality," as foreshadowed in the 1865 resolutions.

> This is indeed a grand conception, which if developed into fact, will immortalize the name of Britain as the most generous and enlightened nation that has adorned the face of the globe.[23]

20. Ibid. xi.
21. Quoted by Donald H. Simpson in "Charles Dickens and the Empire," in *Royal Commonwealth Society Library Notes*, no. 163 (July 1970), p. 16.
22. R. F. Burton, *Wanderings in West Africa* (London, 1863), vol. ii, p. 7.
23. Horton, *West African Countries,* 65.

Nevertheless, he understood clearly that the committee members were not motivated by idealism. He knew that they were not concerned primarily with encouraging African capabilities or with "setting on foot the nationality of a race down-trodden for ages." Their first aim was to be rid of a few burdensome, disease-ridden colonies. He realized that the resolutions would not go far if merely left on paper, and that without a practical policy of African self-help they would be forgotten. The British had taken the initiative, but the response had to come from Africa: "from her sons, and her sons alone, must her complete regeneration be looked for."[24]

He took the four colonies and their hinterlands in turn, evaluating how ready each was for self-government, suggesting practical measures of reform, and outlining a blueprint for future constitutional development.

Sierra Leone, which the committee was least ready to relinquish, he saw as the most ready for self-government. The economy was prospering, and it had an educated population among whom "a *national* spirit" was developing. He proposed it be constituted a monarchy[25] with a king elected by universal suffrage, and a legislature of two houses—a popularly elected House of Assembly with membership restricted to property-owners, a restriction already abolished in 1858 in Britain, and a senate with members chosen by the king. For a short transitional period the king might rule as a governor, under a British governor-in-chief, to gain experience. To make the tiny state economically viable, the surrounding countries would need to be annexed and developed.

A long list of necessary reforms followed. Government should take over full responsibility for education, making it compulsory, founding secondary schools and a teacher training college, and building up Fourah Bay College into a University of West Africa. Export agriculture should be encouraged and new plants introduced. He wanted sanitary and public health reforms, with

24. Ibid. 65-66, 69, 246.
25. Henry Wilson has commented on Horton's deliberately attaching the "respectable labels," monarchy and republic, familiar in Europe, to his proposed states. *Origins of West African Nationalism* (London, 1969), 31.

the medical authorities registering births, deaths and diseases, to establish how healthy or unhealthy the country really was. He proposed a National Bank, municipal government for Freetown, and a programme of public works—a dry dock, piped water, and public parks.

To pay for them, he proposed that the government issue strictly limited amounts of short-term redeemable paper currency, thus avoiding the burden of regular interest payments incurred by national loans. Hence he concluded, "under the fostering care of the mother Government the people can, within a short time, be left to govern themselves."

The Gambia he felt could not become self-governing for another 200 years. But "if radical reform be made," he believed it possible in twenty-five. The main obstacles to development he saw as the lack of education, high death and disease rates, and involvement in the "Marabout-Soninke" wars, with consequent fluctuations in public revenue. Here too he proposed that a king be elected by universal suffrage; no legislature was mentioned, though. The king should develop education, agriculture, and public health, make Bathurst a municipality, and build forts on the frontier, concentrating the villagers in the protected area into defensible towns. To increase trade, the frontier should be extended 200 miles up the river, with a colonial steamer to keep it in touch with Bathurst.

The Gold Coast, with its elite of "scholars" and unexploited natural resources, he saw as readier for self-government. But here too there were obstacles—particularly the division of the coastal region into many small rival kingdoms, and the permanent threat from Ashanti. He proposed it be grouped into two large states, corresponding roughly with the distinction of Fanti and Ga.

Originally, in his *Political Economy*, he had proposed that each state be ruled by one of the traditional kings. Now he preferred that in the west the kings elect an educated man as head king—and suggested George Kuntu Blankson, a wealthy Fanti trader at Anomabu, who was a member of the Colony's Legislative Council. This head king was to rule with a council representing the lower kings and the "scholars" over a united Fanti kingdom. During the transitional stage the British government should supervise, and afterwards a British consul give advice, and protection against European enemies. So united, he believed they could withstand Ashanti; otherwise it might be better for them to come at once under Ashanti rule, barbarous though he considered it to be.

The many small kingdoms of the east he wanted to abolish altogether and unite them as the Republic of Accra. According to his plan, the British government was to nominate an educated man—he suggested Lebrecht Hesse, a magistrate and prominent citizen of Accra[26]—for election as president, to rule for at least an eight-year term, with popularly elected councillors to assist him. As in the west, he proposed a transitional stage under British supervision, with a British consul afterwards. In both states the rulers would have to stimulate education and develop the unused agricultural and mineral potential, to create a stable economic base for two prosperous unified nations.

He wrote little about Lagos. He was chiefly concerned to justify the British annexation of 1861, and to show that it must be retained as "a star from which must radiate the refulgent rays of civilization into the interior." But he did suggest a few practical reforms—improving the city drainage, developing water transport, and building tramways to carry produce from the interior.

He wrote more fully on the Yoruba interior, describing it as "the kingdom of the Akus": in Sierra Leone the Yoruba were called "Aku," from their way of greeting one another. The word "kingdom" was here misleading. As he explained, the former kingdom of Oyo, or "Yoruba," as he called it, which had once united them, had broken up some fifty years earlier, and the smaller, rival successor states had been fighting one another intermittently ever since. One reason why he wanted Lagos to remain British was that he hoped British influence would bring the Yoruba together and end the bitter civil wars. As elsewhere, he envisioned educated African Christians transforming the Yoruba states into modern nations. As an example of this process already happening, he cited the Egba United Board of Management, created at Abeokuta by a returned Sierra Leonean, G. W. Johnson.

26. There is an obituary of Hesse in *Gold Coast Times,* July 31, 1874.

He concluded with a country still remote from British rule, though beginning to come under Christian influence—his parents' own Ibo homeland. He called it the "Empire of the Eboes (Iboes, Igboes, Egboes)," giving the variant renderings used by contemporary writers. He did not explain why he used the label "empire" for a collection of small, jealously independent states, united only by "one national sentiment."

His description was based on published accounts. He may have added information from his own upbringing by Ibo parents, but if so, he did not say so. He relied chiefly on two recently published books, one by Dr. William Baikie, the other by Bishop Crowther and the Reverend J. C. Taylor. Baikie had returned from a voyage up the Niger in 1854 (calling in at Freetown a few months before Horton left for England) and published his *Narrative* in 1856. Crowther and Taylor, Taylor was an Ibo descendant, had then founded the Niger Mission, and in 1859 published an edited version of their journals, depicting the Ibo very favourably.[27]

Baikie declared, "The religion of the Igbo is entirely Pagan." Horton came to a different conclusion. "The religion of the Egboes is Judaism, intermixed with numerous pagan rites and ceremonies." He quoted from Crowther and Taylor to show similarities between Ibo theology and worship and those of the Old Testament Jews, hazarding the theory of a Jewish dispersion over Africa.

This claim had already been made in a book he did not mention, and presumably did not know, the *Interesting Narrative* published in London in 1789 by Olaudah Equiano (or Gustavus Vassa), the first book published in England by an Ibo.[28] It had been taken up in 1865 in a letter to the *African Times* entitled "Black, the Original Colour of the White Race" which Horton quoted from in his book. (The letter was signed "H." so it is possible that he might have written it himself). The writer was

27. William Baikie, *Narrative of an Exploring Voyage* (London, 1856); S. A. Crowther and J. C. Taylor, *Journals and Notices of the Native Missionaries accompanying the Niger Expedition of 1857-59* (London, 1859).
28. Reprinted in 1969 with comprehensive introduction and annotations by Paul Edwards.

concerned primarily to show that it could be inferred from the location of the Garden of Eden that the first man was dark skinned, but he went on to suggest that the Ibo might turn out to be "the offspring of the lost tribes of Israel."

Always interested in geology, he quoted reports suggesting that the Ibo country might be rich in gold and other minerals, and looked forward to the greater development of agricultural produce for export. He considered carefully how to turn the many disunited Ibo states into "an independent, united, Christian and civilized nation." His solution, as elsewhere, was a united kingdom: he did not apparently realize that kingship was rare among the Ibo. He proposed that the Ibo kings and chiefs elect a supreme king to rule from a seacoast capital, preferably Bonny, with some kind of advisory council. To keep his kingdom together, he would have to raise a standing army and introduce a common currency with his own mint.

Eventually Horton envisioned a strong united Ibo state, emerging through the industry and enterprise of its people. Education, which should be compulsory (it was not yet compulsory in Britain), would be in the hands of missionaries, preferably of the Basel mission, for he again insisted that,

> It is impossible for a nation to civilize itself; civilization must come from abroad. As was the case with the civilized continents of Europe and America, so it must be with Africa.[29]

He also looked beyond the separate nations to a united West Africa. Ultimately he wanted to see a general Legislative Assembly for all the coast (a constitution was sketched out for it in his *Political Economy*). His university was to be a University of West Africa, and he recommended a unified educational system. Hence George Shepperson has claimed him as one of the pioneers of "pan-Africanism."[30] Like many pan-Africans he seems to have felt himself most an African outside Africa. It was in Edinburgh that he adopted the name "Africanus." And towards the end of his life, speaking in London on a non-political

29. Horton, *West African Countries*, 175.
30. Introduction to the second edition of *West African Countries*, xvi-xvii.

subject (gold mining), he began with the words, "Being an African and loving my country . . ."[31]

His constitution-making followed a consistent pattern: a strong ruler was to unify and develop the nation. Though he allowed for representative or advisory institutions, he plainly meant his kings and presidents to rule with authority. They were to do what they thought best for their countries. He had no use for party politics. His states were to strive for consensus. He called upon the people to consider only their country's interest, "and thus their interest and that of their Government will not clash, but become identical."[32]

This authoritarian approach is not surprising. He had grown up under the paternal rule of a colonial government that he believed to be basically benevolent. He had been educated within the authoritarian structure of a missionary society whose agents were under orders. He was himself an army officer, accustomed to give orders and be obeyed. As a doctor he regularly told other people what to do, for what he believed was their own good.

He expressed his feelings more explicitly in a later book,

in the government of a semi-barbarous race . . . *a little despotism is absolutely necessary* . . . having this object in view—*the material advancement of the people.*[33]

In that book he also expressed his admiration for the no-nonsense methods adopted in West Africa by the French (whose then ruler, Emperor Napoleon III, had been elected by universal suffrage, like his proposed king of Sierra Leone).

Hence his envisioned governments were unashamedly paternal, with powers to compel their peoples to improve themselves—rebuild their houses, re-plan their towns, submit their children to education—state interference to an extent that was not yet tolerable in Britain in 1868. "It is the duty of a civilized government to endeavour as much as in it lies to civilize the natives under its rule." Above all, they were to stimulate their peoples to

31. *Journal of the Royal Society of Arts*, vol. xxx (1881-82), p. 782.
32. Horton, *West African Countries*, 249.
33. Horton, *Letters*, 138.

develop the natural resources of their countries on a large scale. Horton realized clearly that this was no easy task.

> . . . in England the labouring class has always great external pressure to bear upon them, demanding both their moral and their physical strength; whilst the same class in Africa has little or no external pressure to bear on them. In England the food of the peasant is compound, expensive and very scarce; in Africa the food is simple, cheap and plentiful. In England the peasant is compelled by the state of civilization and the necessity of the climate to procure clothing, which entails a greater outlay and a necessity for increased labour; but in Africa the climate is so hot and uniform that the peasants go about half naked, and therefore have little or no expense for clothing.
>
> Now with all these local advantages on the side of the African peasantry can it be a matter of surprise that they confine themselves almost entirely to the cultivation of produce sufficient for their yearly consumption? Can it be a matter of surprise, I say, that the English peasant labours infinitely more than the African peasant? In the one case the land supplies the peasant abundantly, whether he works hard or not; in the other, starvation awaits him if he does not work hard, and should he not pay dearly with his strength and skill, he is sure to fall to utter destitution. To the English peasant the words of Mr Thomas Carlyle, in his inaugural address as Lord Rector of Edinburgh University, echo loudly. "If a man," says he, "gets meat and clothes, what matters it whether he have ten thousand pounds, or ten million pounds, or seventy pounds a-year? He can get meat and clothes for that, and he will find very little real difference intrinsically, *if he is a wise man.*"[34]

Just as he used Burton's travel data when it suited him, he here quoted another notorious negrophobe, Thomas Carlyle, to reinforce his argument.[35] But he and Carlyle, whatever wisdom they might ascribe to the contented peasant, both believed in a higher wisdom—the gospel of repressive hard work and ceaseless competition, and the sacred duty of putting natural resources to their most productive use for the benefit of mankind. Horton believed that the West African countries could never develop into modern nations unless they were radically reorganized. To raise the revenue to pay for the reorganization, their economies would have to be switched from subsistence to export. Such a change would demand a social as well as an economic revolution,

34. Horton, *West African Countries,* 199.
35. Carlyle was Rector of Edinburgh University 1865–66.

and could only be carried out if the people were re-educated for it.

Hence he saw education as an indispensable part of development. In his "Vindication" chapters he had argued that education was the key to free Africans from the racists' prison of allegedly permanent inferiority. He now argued that it was the key to open up the unused potential of West Africa. He was convinced that only education could free people from the unenterprising ways that kept their countries economically stagnant. He therefore insisted that governments must undertake the responsibility of providing education for every child in the country. They would have to spend money unproductively, as an investment, not just to breed small literate elites, but to train up whole populations of industrious, educated people.

These dynamic policies demanded large government expenditure—substantial investment for the sake of future return. But here he was going against the whole trend of British rule in West Africa. British colonial policy paid occasional lip-service to development. But a tradition of official parsimony restricted public expenditure to the minimum necessary to keep administration going. If import-export trade brought in enough customs revenue to balance the budget the Colonial Office was contented. During Horton's lifetime, and in the imperial era that followed, the colonial governments were to spend very little to develop West Africa.[36]

Nor did African nationalists in the generations after his death take up his demands for economic development. They feared that if their countries were developed under colonial rule, expatriate entrepreneurs would get all the profit, and would rob the people of their land. They put political action before economic. Indeed most pan-African leaders have tended to look back to a romanticized African past rather than forward to a

36. Sir Gordon Guggisberg, an Englishman who governed the Gold Coast from 1919-29, was almost alone in introducing large-scale educational and economic development policies into British West Africa. Like Horton, he had been an army officer in one of the professional branches of the service (a surveyor), and was energetic, far-sighted, and paternalistic (R. E. Wraith, *Guggisberg*, London, 1967).

modernized African future.[37] Not until the 1940's and 1950's, when British rule in Africa was drawing to an end, did governments and people begin to take seriously what Horton had been preaching seventy or eighty years before.

PHYSICAL AND MEDICAL CLIMATE

Horton's *Physical and Medical Climate and Meteorology of the West Coast of Africa* was written in Africa: the preface was dated from the Gambia, October 1866. It was published by John Churchill, who had published his *Medical Topography,* and appeared in October 1867, just after he arrived in England.

He wrote it as a reference book for West Africa, to match similar books that had appeared on India and Ceylon. As he observed, Europeans were always asserting unquestioningly that it was a deadly area, but without ever having considered systematically why, or even whether, this was so. Constant changes of station, whatever harm they had done to his health, had given his a wide experience which enabled him to write with knowledge and authority.

In his presentation he was guided by a standard work, *The Influence of Tropical Climates,* by Sir Ranald Martin, a distinguished army doctor who had served in India, though he did not always necessarily agree with Martin's theories. Like Martin, he assumed that there was a correlation between physical environment, disease, and human behaviour. This, as we have seen, was also the basis of his theory of race. But he was not content merely to describe. Practical as always, he demanded medical and sanitary reform. Development of the type he envisioned required a healthy as well as an educated population, for disease checked "the progress of true civilization in tropical countries." Though primarily a medical book, it also had a political message.

As in *West African Countries,* he displayed an impressive range of reading, quoting from medical books, journals, and official reports, which he must have carried about with him from one station to another. He mentioned—while considering the effect of

37. Imanuel Geiss, *Panafrikanismus* (Frankfurt, 1968), 122, 162, 328.

heat on human performance—that whereas in England he had managed to study fourteen hours a day without discomfort, in West Africa he could not manage more than six.[38] But plainly he put his six daily hours to good use. He included statistical material—tables of meteorological readings, mostly taken by himself, and of mortality, from official sources—but realized that they were too unsystematic and covered too narrow a range to be comprehensive. In any cast, his own readings had been restricted because his barometer had been accidentally destroyed.

He organized his material by topics, considering in turn the effect of sun, wind, elevation, soil, rainfall, etc., on each locality. Though the arrangement might confuse a reader interested in any one particular locality, it drove home a general message. In one chapter after another, he showed that the coastal West African towns were in urgent need of sanitary reform. In England in his day sanitation was belatedly being taken seriously; Florence Nightingale was calling official attention to the fearful sanitary problems of the cities of India. Yet it was hard to turn public attention to a subject that most respectable people still found distasteful. As he remarked, the outbreak of an epidemic might arouse them to panic, but once it was over apathy soon succeeded.[39]

The sanitary reforms he had proposed in his *Political Economy* had been ill received by readers in West Africa. Yet he persisted, depicting particularly the insanitary condition of Freetown and Bathurst, inadequately sited and drained, without a piped water supply, or public sewage disposal. He painted a terrifying picture. Tons of human and animal waste were deposited annually, contaminating the soil, water, and air. He produced statistics to show that if the present mortality rate in Bathurst continued, the whole population would die out within fifty years. As an immediate palliative measure, he urged those who could afford it to move to healthier areas—from Bathurst towards the sea and from Freetown into the mountains.[40]

His medical conclusions assumed that diseases were dependent

38. Horton, *Physical and Medical Climate,* 68.
39. Ibid. vi.
40. Ibid. 76-82, 267-68.

on season and climate: hence his close attention to weather conditions and physical environment. From his student days he had been interested in malaria. In his doctoral thesis he mentioned that he was proposing to publish an "Etiology of Tropical Malaria" in which he would consider "the effect of clayey soil in engendering disease." Like most contemporaries he believed that malaria and yellow fever were caused by breathing in poisonous vapour that rose from the soil, and quoted Shakespeare in support of it.[41] He was therefore concerned to purify the environment, without realizing that it was not the stagnant pools, but the mosquitoes that bred in them, that spread the disease. Not until he had been dead sixteen years did Sir Ronald Ross's experiments in Freetown conclusively prove the mosquito theory.

His own theories about the control of malaria had been shaped by his experiences at Keta, where he had concluded that large trees, particularly coconut trees, reduce its incidence. He recommended large-scale planting in swampy neighbourhoods, particularly near towns. He contrasted Cape Coast, well planted with shady trees, with Freetown, where, at this period, there were still no trees planted in the streets, and with Lagos, where there were not enough.

His experiments at Keta had convinced him of the efficacy of another preventative agent, "nature's universal disinfectant, *ozone*." He observed that malaria was most prevalent at the onset of the rainy season, a period when the amount of ozone in the atmosphere was low, and was less prevalent in dry weather, at times when the air was charged with electricity by thunderstorms. Hence he inferred that "the quantity of ozone in the atmosphere has an indisputable effect on the influence of fever in malarious districts.[42] To establish his theory he manufactured "ozonometers"—papers covered with iodide of potassium and starch, which discoloured according to the amount of ozone in the atmosphere. He quoted Australian experiments which indicated that ozone might be used as a general disinfectant to purify the air, and looked forward to the discovery of a means for creating

41. Ibid. 105.
42. Ibid. 220.

and preserving it artificially on a large scale, to be "continually used in places where malaria is continually generated."[43]

Though he was mistaken in relating malaria and ozone, his experiments at Keta established something that was not yet accepted—that people living beside the sea can catch malaria. Even after the mosquito theory had been proved, this was still denied. Eventually it was shown that the malaria-carrying *anopheles Gambiae melas* can breed beside salt water. Horton's observations therefore were right, though his deductions were wrong.[44]

At the end of the book he included hints for Europeans going to the tropics, mostly adapted from standard works written for India. He recommended them to lead temperate abstemious lives, to wear cotton clothes, to eat and drink moderately but well, to avoid brandy, bottled beer, and licentious indulgences, and not to take violent exercise. Warned no doubt by the idle vicious lives he had seen his brother officers leading, he recommended, "always keep the mind occupied in doing something; never sit down and allow the thoughts to go astray"—advice that this industrious officer, always busy with some project or another, certainly followed himself.

In this section, which is headed "Regulation of the Passions," he continued,

> agreable society should always be courted, as it relieves the mind a great deal. The society of real ladies will be found preferable to any other.

GUINEA WORM

Horton's *Guinea Worm, or Dracunculus* is a 51-page study of a debilitating parasitic body worm prevalent in tropical countries. He had practical reasons for his study: one-third of the soldiers admitted to hospital in the Gold Coast were suffering from it. There was already a substantial body of learned description and theorizing, chiefly based on research in India, for him to draw on. It had been described in its West African setting by James Lynd, an eighteenth-century pioneer of British tropical medicine, and

43. Ibid. 233.
44. Davidson Nicol, *Africanus Horton* (London, 1969), 149.

in two medical books on Sierra Leone—Thomas Winterbottom's *Account*, published in 1803, and Robert Clarke's *Sierra Leone*, published in 1846. Heinrich Barth, the great German traveller, depicted a guinea worm in his journals, and also guessed correctly how it was transmitted to human beings. Even Burton put a footnote on it into his *Wanderings*.

It was disputed by scientists whether the parasite was transmitted into the human body internally, through drinking water, or externally, by contact with the skin. Horton and most contemporaries believed incorrectly that it was transmitted by contact. However the year after his book appeared, a Russian scientist observed that when the guinea worm larva reached water it was absorbed into a minute parasitic host which, if swallowed, transmitted the guinea worm into humans. The actual process of transmission was only worked out in the twentieth century, partly by another West African scientist, Sanya Onabamiro.[45]

Horton began with a description of the parasite and the symptoms of its appearance in the human body. Then followed six case studies of his own patients. He went on to argue the case for transmission by contact, adding as his own hypothesis the possibility of transmission through another infected person, as well as (what was generally believed) through the soil. As always, he put his research into the wider perspective of climate and geology: he believed infection to be most prevalent during the rainy and harmattan seasons (less so in hot, dry weather), and in places with a volcanic soil. He suggested a further correlation, based on his own observations at Dixcove, between susceptibility to guinea worm and susceptibility to elephantiasis.

He concluded with diagnosis and treatment. As palliatives he recommended poultices, mentioning an African plant which he had heard was effectively used, but had not tried himself. For radical treatment he recommended *assafoetida*, a nauseous drink, which he declared killed the parasite quickly and gave permanent relief.

45. Sir Philip Manson-Bahr (ed.), *Manson's Tropical Diseases* (London, 1960), 771-78, 1020-23; *The British Encyclopedia of Medical Practice* (London, 1951), vol. vi, p. 101; Ibid. *Cumulative Supplement, 1969-70*, pp. 402-3. I am grateful to Dr. Davidson Nicol for help with these references.

The book was written, or perhaps finished, in England in 1867. Churchill published it in 1868. It was dedicated to the Director-General of the Army Medical Department, Dr. (later Sir) T. G. Logan.

On his return to duty he had the opportunity of doing more research on the guinea worm, when he found it was attacking the soldiers in the Accra garrison. He wrote a short report which was included as a two-page appendix in the Army Medical Department Annual Report for 1870. He emphasized here what he had only suggested in the book, that guinea worm tends to be endemic where, as in Accra, the soil is volcanic.[46]

BOOK REVIEWS

Horton's writings were well advertised in the *African Times,* with long extracts from the *Political Economy,* a favourable review reprinted from the *Hastings and St Leonards News,* and enthusiastic reviews of *Physical and Medical Climate* and *West African Countries.* In this way they were made known to the West African reading public. *West African Countries* was advertised for sale in all four British colonies by mid-1868, making it possible to fulfill Fitzgerald's recommendation that "this book ought to be read and studied by all educated Africans." Next year an African correspondent wrote from Fernando Po to say that some members of the European community there had read it, but refused to believe that it could possibly have been written by an African.[47]

In return for this publicity Horton subscribed to a book Fitzgerald published in 1868, *The Course of Divine Love,* an ecstatic, sanctimonious, but unavailing plea to the British public to pour out money to benefit Africa (which anticipated the aid programmes of the 1950's and 1960's).

The British medical press welcomed *Physical and Medical Climate* as an original and useful contribution to medical knowledge—though the reviewer in *The Lancet* felt that the mass of descriptive detail about West Africa detracted from its value as a

46. Parliamentary Papers, 1870, vol. xliii, pp. 335-36.
47. *African Times,* June 23, 1868, Sept. 23, 1868, Dec. 23, 1869.

medical work. *The Athenaeum,* a London journal devoted to "literature, science and the fine arts," gave it a long favourable notice.[48] *West African Countries and Peoples* aroused less interest. Those ready to take note when an African wrote about medicine were apparently less interested in his political opinions. *The Record,* a Church newspaper, commented favourably, noting the dedication to Venn and concluding, "To Christian philanthropists the practical lesson of Dr. Horton's book is '*Persevere.*' " But the influential political and literary journals—the *Edinburgh Review,* the *Quarterly Review,* the *Fortnightly Review, Blackwoods Magazine*—ignored it.

In these books Horton had answered overwhelmingly the "False Theories of Modern Anthropologists" (a chapter-heading from *West African Countries and Peoples*). He had shown that an African was capable of observing and theorizing as a physical and political scientist, and of embodying original conclusions in lucid intelligent prose. This "Vindication of the African Race" answered those who asserted that Africans were incapable of creating anything—unless, indeed, they chose the weapon of silence, ignored his writings and achievements, and expelled him from their consciousness into oblivion.

48. *The Lancet,* Feb. 1, 1868; *The Athenaeum,* Nov. 2, 1867.

V

THE FANTI CONFEDERATION

ANGLO–FANTI TENSIONS

HORTON WAS NOT IDLE (was he ever idle?) during his stay in England. He spent much of it at the Royal Victoria Hospital, Netley, the Army Medical School. There, as well as doing his own writing, he attended medical lectures. In the hospital museum he came upon a sealed jar containing laterite soil, sent there three years earlier from Sierra Leone by one of his army medical colleagues. He analysed it, and had the pleasure of seeing his two-page analysis appear in the appendix to the Army Medical Department Report for 1868.[1] These reports were prepared annually and printed for Parliament. To have research notes included in them (and his account of the Accra guinea worm outbreak appeared in 1870) was something most medical officers never achieved.

He then moved to London, where he stayed in Pentonville Road. During his stay he bought from the widow of a former official of the Court of Mixed Commission in Sierra Leone, a substantial house in Gloucester Street, Freetown. It had been erected about twenty-five years earlier and covered three town lots, stretching back into Charlotte Street. It cost him £600. He named it "Horton Hall."[2]

1. Parliamentary Papers, 1867-68, vol. xliv, pp. 333-34.
2. Registrar-General's Office, Freetown, Conveyance Book, vol. 31, p. 134, conveyance dated June 16, 1868.

Before leaving London he attended a royal levee at St James's Palace, where he was presented to the Prince of Wales.[3] More important, he called on Edward Cardwell, the Secretary of State for War, and presented him with a copy of *West African Countries and Peoples*. He acknowledged in Cardwell's contribution to the 1865 resolutions the starting point of his own political proposals, and had already dedicated his *Physical and Medical Climate* to him. On the strength of their meeting in London, he was to send him the series of letters which were published in 1870 as *Letters on the Political Condition of the Gold Coast*.

In August 1868 he returned to Cape Coast and once again was sent off to outstations. During the next twelve months he was twice in Lagos. There, as well as his medical and military routine, he had exacting administrative duties, as he was put in charge of military stores and supplies, and was responsible for all money passing through the department.[4] For a while he was in Accra (observing guinea worm among other activities). In May 1869 cholera broke out in the Gambia and he was sent to reinforce the medical authorities. But the worst was over by the time he arrived and he returned in about a month.[5] By August he was back at Cape Coast again, writing the first of his letters to Cardwell.

The British forts had governments of the usual colonial pattern—a governor ruling with an Executive and a Legislative Council. Strictly, this government ruled only the forts. But the "Bonds" made with the coastal rulers emboldened some governors to treat the surrounding country as if it were a British protectorate. In 1852 the rulers had been persuaded to levy a poll tax on their subjects, receiving salaries out of the tax money. Their peoples objected; at Accra they resisted forcibly and a British naval ship bombarded the town. Eventually the tax had to be abandoned. This episode discredited the colonial adminis-

3. *African Times,* June 23, 1868.
4. *West African Reporter,* Jan. 15, 1881; *Lagos Eagle & Critic,* Nov. 24, 1883.
5. J. A. B. Horton, *The Diseases of Tropical Climates and their Treatment,* 2nd ed. (London, 1879), 312. It was 101 years before cholera again appeared in West Africa.

tration; as a result, the 1865 committee were told, "faith in the white man on the coast is very much shaken."[6]

During the 1860's relations between Africans and Europeans grew steadily worse. Underlying all disputes was one basic misunderstanding—the extent of British authority. Horton put the legal position succinctly: "beyond the Fort-gate we have not a foot of ground in the country."[7] The influence exercised beyond the forts was not based on British sovereignty, but on agreements, the "Bonds," made with independent sovereign states.

Most British officials refused to admit that the coastal states were still independent. They assumed that the peoples in the "Protectorate," as they called it, must regard them as superiors, and would be obedient and loyal to Britain. But, as Francis Agbodeka has observed, "what the British mistook for loyalty was in fact admiration."[8] Admiration was already soured by the poll tax episode. After the humiliating Ashanti war of 1863–64, when the British authorities abandoned the allegedly "protected" peoples to the mercy of their enemies, it faded away completely. Having once freely accepted voluntary agreements, the coastal rulers felt they could as freely repudiate them.

This the British, on the coast and in London, would not admit. Yet there was no general agreement about what rights (if any) they could legally exercise in the "Protectorate." Policy varied with each successive governor. Turnover among governors was rapid. Between 1862 and 1867, as Horton angrily noted, no less than seven held office, each with his own policy.

In 1866, on the recommendation of the 1865 committee, the four British West African possessions were united under the name of the West African Settlements. A governor-in-chief was appointed, to reside in Sierra Leone, and pay only occasional visits along the coast. In each subordinate settlement an administrator was in charge, responsible to the governor-in-chief, and corresponding with the Colonial Office through him.

6. David Kimble, *A Political History of Ghana* (London, 1963), 189.
7. Horton, *West African Countries*, 219.
8. Francis Agbodeka, "The Fanti Confederacy 1865–69," *Transactions of the Historical Society of Ghana*, vol. vii (1964), 105.

Horton welcomed the change, hoping that unified government would bring vigorous, consistent policy-making, the kind he approved of. He liked Sir Arthur Kennedy, a former governor of Sierra Leone, who was appointed governor-in-chief in 1868—an energetic paternalist, who deliberately appointed and promoted Africans to senior government posts. In practice, however, policy-making suffered. Decisions were delayed even more than in the past. The administrator had to refer all important matters to his immediate superior in Freetown, and with this extension of the chain of command, British policy in the Gold Coast became less, not more, vigorous and consistent.

Discontent among the Fanti and other coastal peoples was not confined to rulers. In the coastal states the power structure was gradually changing. The urban *asafo,* the untitled freemen, and—far more important—those who had received a European type of education, were gaining more political power. Not only the wealthy import-export merchants of Cape Coast, Anomabu, and Accra, but many others, with a smattering of literacy, could claim status as "scholars." They shared the political grievances felt by their non-literate relatives, and could formulate them in ways Europeans could understand.

Nevertheless British officials refused to accept the claims of these educated Africans to represent their people. Many followed Burton in resenting their very existence. Though British policy allowed the appointment of Africans to government posts, Horton's career illustrated the difficulties that confronted an African official. Educated Africans, often described as "half-educated"—a formulation which implied that only a European could be fully educated—were made scapegoats to explain failures of policy.

Governor after governor maintained that the coastal peoples and their rulers would be perfectly satisfied with British policy, if only they were not stirred up into protest by seditious literates. This deep-rooted belief—that African peoples are happy under European rule unless incited against it by literate agitators—was to become the mainstay of European rule in Africa, and lingers still wherever white supremacy remains on the continent.

Racial theories were invoked, too. Some of the "scholars" were of part-European descent, members of families into which a

European trader or missionary had once married. A few were West Indians. Such "mulattos" could be smeared in terms of current racial assumptions as inherently immoral and degenerate. Governor Kennedy, who was ready to favour Africans, mistrusted anyone of mixed descent. His successor, Governor Hennessy (who was deeply impressed by Blyden's racial theories), shared his preference for "pure Negroes." Thus any African with European affinities, whether of descent or of education, was potentially suspect.

No wonder British officials hated Ferdinand Fitzgerald and his *African Times*, which gave literate Africans the means of airing their grievances publicly. What they refused to see was that these grievances were often widely shared by those unable to express them on paper, and that the rulers, the educated, and the people formed one community.

The Fanti, fragmented and disunited, were coming to see that they must unite in opposition to the longstanding Ashanti threat, and the new threat from the British. All through the mid-1860's there were movements to repudiate British encroachments. The most spectacular was at Cape Coast, where King John Aggrey openly declared that the jurisdictions being exercised in his country were illegal. The *African Times* publicized his case. But neither the administrator, H. T. Ussher, nor the Colonial Office would admit his claims. Ussher merely blamed his educated advisers, and eventually deposed him.

In the eastern districts, too, the peoples were coming together. The three kings of the traditional divisions of Accra (British, Dutch, and Danish), who had established authority over the peoples inland, questioned and defied instructions from the British administration. The Accra merchants, a substantial, well-educated group, supported them. Right across the "Protectorate" British claims were being contested.

THE FANTI CONFEDERATION

A perennial source of European weakness on the Gold Coast was the close proximity of the British and Dutch forts. Forts jostled one another all along the coastline, making it impossible for either government to introduce a workable fiscal policy. If customs duties were imposed at British Accra, ships would merely call in at Dutch Accra next door.

By the mid-nineteenth century the Dutch government had virtually written off its possessions. Once the slave trade ceased they had gone into rapid decline. Expenditure was cut to a minimum. Import-export trade was small. Even the Ashanti traded more through Cape Coast than Elmina, which was more a political than an economic asset for the Asantahene.[9]

From time to time over the decades proposals had been put forward for rationalizing the British and Dutch spheres, by grouping them together into two coherent units divided by the Kakum (Sweet) river. The British would have Cape Coast and eastward including Accra; the Dutch would have Elmina and westward including Dixcove. The growing political difficulties made such a solution increasingly attractive to British and Dutch officials on the coast. In London however, in the era of the 1865 resolutions, some people preferred to discuss handing over all the British forts to the Dutch.

One insuperable legal difficulty stood in the way of this plan. The Dutch, whatever they might say, had no sovereignty over their possessions. The British had sovereignty only over the forts. Neither had any authority to fix a frontier at the Kakum river or anywhere else. But this was brushed aside as a technicality. As in the European partition of Africa later in the century, the African populations were not consulted. By a treaty signed in 1867 between the British and Dutch governments they were transferred—as they felt, like slaves—from one European power to another. And the treaty even contained a preamble claiming that it had been made "to promote the interests of the inhabitants"—the appeal to a self-appointed white man's right to determine what was best for Africa that was to echo through the treaties of the Scramble period.

In the eastern districts the Dutch forts were transferred peacefully. But in the west the Fanti were enraged that a British

9. Douglas Coombs, *The Gold Coast, Britain and the Netherlands, 1850–74* (London, 1963), 129. This book gives the background and details of the Anglo-Dutch negotiations.

government to whom they owed no allegiance should hand them over to the Dutch, the traditional allies of their Ashanti enemies. Fanti dreams of unity suddenly became a reality. In January 1868 some of the leading chiefs and educated Fanti met at Mankessim, their traditional centre of religious allegiance, to form a Fanti Council, or, as it was later to be called, Confederation.

While they were deliberating, they heard that a Dutch warship had bombarded Kommenda, a seaport where the people had refused to accept the transfer. The news stirred the remaining Fanti to join. In Horton's words, "the Fantee race flew to arms," marched against the Dutch, and beseiged Elmina. Their immediate aim was to force the Dutch out of West Africa. Their ultimate aim was to supersede the British, who, as Horton pointed out, had envisioned in 1865 the transfer of power to such a government as the Confederation foreshadowed.[10]

No British administrator, however, was prepared to see the Confederation in this way. Ussher could only see it as he had seen Aggrey's protest—a hostile, unauthorized threat to his authority. As before, he blamed the "mulattoes and semi-educated blacks" whom he believed were behind it. As long as the Fanti Confederation lasted, Ussher and the administrators who succeeded him subjected its leaders to petty annoyances and humiliations, and did all they could to suppress it.

Governor Kennedy was more sympathetic. He understood the nascent nationalism behind the movement. On a visit late in 1868 he met its leaders and was favourably impressed. But normally he was far off in Freetown. Whatever the regulations might prescribe, it was the man on the spot whose influence counted. In any case his sympathy gradually faded away. In Freetown he antagonized an influential West Indian lawyer of part-African descent, William Rainy, who was friendly with Fitzgerald. The *African Times* which, like Horton, had begun by praising Kennedy, ended by attacking him. As Fitzgerald was a champion of the Fanti Confederation, Kennedy turned against it, on the principle of guilt by association. Always a vindictive, unscru-

10. Horton, *Letters,* 21, 27-28.

pulous fighter, who habitually used his despatches to the Colonial Office to smear his opponents, he changed his tone. The Fanti leaders, whom he had formerly praised, now became "self-seeking mulattoes" and men "devoid of education, means or character."[11]

Horton began his series of letters on the political situation on 12 August 1868, addressing the first three to Cardwell, the rest to the Secretary of State for the Colonies, Lord Granville. They were received at the Colonial Office like any other official correspondence, and were minuted on by the officials, who found them "able and temperate." One of them expressed surprise: "I was not prepared to hear that he was a negro."[12] The letters began with the disastrous results of the Dutch transfer treaty, and continued by looking back to the Ashanti war of 1863–64. Then followed a month by month narrative of events until May 1870. Throughout he stressed the importance of the Fanti Confederation, now working towards that "Self-government of the Gold Coast" which he had dreamed of in *West African Countries and Peoples*.

He had proposed a united Fanti kingdom, under one king, ruling with a representative council. Originally (in his *Political Economy*) he had suggested King Aggrey of Cape Coast, but after Aggrey's deposition he substituted George Blankson, an educated Fanti commoner. At Mankessim, rival Fanti kings disputed for precedence, and a compromise version of his proposal was adopted. Instead of a king, a Chief Magistrate, Richard John Ghartey, a self-educated businessman from Winneba, was appointed, and subsequently he became President of the Fanti Confederation. George Blankson, Jr., whose father Horton had wanted for king, was secretary; when he died, another prominent Anomabu man, J. H. Brew, succeeded him.

The Fanti Confederation established the apparatus of a recognized government. Ghartey heard legal cases from the Fanti constituent states. A poll tax was collected to provide revenue, but it was not merely an instrument of government. Its sponsors

11. P.R.O., C.O. 96/92, Kennedy, Jan. 2, 1872; C.O. 96/89, Kennedy, 152, Dec. 16, 1871.
12. The letters are in P.R.O., C.O. 96/83, 85, 86; for minutes quoted by Barrow and Herbert, see C.O. 96/85, Kennedy, 62, June 10, 1870.

followed Horton in hoping to introduce policies of education and economic development. As the Ghanaian historian Magnus Sampson put it, "Ghartey tried to do for the Gold Coast in 1867 what Meiji did for Japan in 1867."[13]

The immediate objective was fighting the Dutch who were joined by a small unofficial Ashanti force. But the Netherlands government was not prepared to go on fighting. It had already had enough of West Africa. The Dutch began negotiations to transfer their possessions to Britain. In London a government ostensibly committed to reducing its West African responsibilities was unenthusiastic. In February 1869 Granville refused to consider the proposal. By October he had changed his mind. It might be that the letters he had received from Horton, who since 1865 had been urging the government to acquire the Dutch forts, contributed to the change.

On 25 February 1871, therefore, a treaty was signed transferring the Dutch forts to Britain. The Fanti Confederation had gained its first objective—driving the Dutch from West Africa.

In the east, too, the peoples of Horton's imagined "Republic of Accra" were moving in the direction he had outlined. Ussher reacted here as in Cape Coast, blaming the educated, and arresting Lebrecht Hesse, who had been Horton's candidate for president—but on a charge so vague that Kennedy had to repudiate the arrest. It was plain to the educated citizens of Accra that they must take the initiative to protect their counry against British encroachments.

James Bannerman (whose brother, Charles, had been one of King Aggrey's advisers) consulted Horton, and in 1869 formed an Accra Native Confederation. William Lutterodt, "the acknowledged head of the educated natives of Accra" was president; Hesse and Bannerman were on the managing committee. The kings of Accra agreed to co-operate. Bannerman told Horton that he intended the confederation to be "the germ of that form of government (Republican) which you have advocated in your book on Western Africa."[14] Horton, therefore, in 1870 could see

13. Magnus J. Sampson, *Gold Coast Men of Affairs* (London, 1937), 14.
14. Horton, *Letters,* 34-41; P.R.O., C.O. 96/81 Kendall, 93, Sept. 17, 1869, enclosures.

in both parts of the country the kinds of development he had proposed only two years earlier being carried out by the inhabitants.

HORTON AND THE CONFEDERATION

Horton finished his letters before the Dutch cession was announced, but he took it for granted that they would move out soon. Yet, despite what he had previously maintained, he did not welcome transfer of the Dutch forts to a British government which had done so little for the country. He declared that he would prefer transfer to the French, whose methods (it may be recalled) he was inclined to admire—even to the Germans, "a hard-working plodding race," who might develop the economy (when he wrote there was still no German Empire in existence, only a North German Confederation). He even welcomed the possibility of German immigration," which would be of great advantage to the country":[15] his welcome will have been tempered by his belief that European populations could not sustain themselves permanently in West Africa.

Turning to the areas under British control, he urged the Secretary of State to appoint only tactful, conciliatory administrators, replace the regular troops by a locally raised militia, and spend far more money on education. He sketched out a plan for government sponsored schools.

But his main emphasis, as thoughout the letters, was on the Fanti Confederation. He analysed Fanti society, as emerging from a feudal system "tottering to its foundation," and saw the Confederation as the agent which would guide its development into a modern state. The British government, which grudged every penny on colonial expenditure, had proved incompetent to develop the country: "education and industrial pursuits have never been encouraged by the authorities on the Coast among the interior tribes, and there is no reason to believe that they ever will be encouraged." Instead, the Fanti Confederation would take over, "so as not only to relieve the Imperial exchequer from its heavy outlay, but also to lessen the awful responsibility of the

15. Horton, *Letters,* 142.

Home Government on matters relating to so distant and un-healthy a colony."[16]

He therefore asked the Secretary of State to recognize the Confederation officially, and treat its members as friendly allies, not as contemptible subversives. With recognition and encourage-ment it would successfully implement the policies of defence, education, and economic development which the British had neglected.

He concluded his letters with a sketch of a formal constitution for the Confederation. He proposed an elected president, min-isters (for internal and external affairs), and a chief justice, with a Confederate Diet of two houses. The kings and principal rulers would sit in the Royal House. The other would be a Represen-tative Assembly, elected by all the citizens. "The fundamental law of the country should guarantee to every citizen equal rights and protection, and direct or indirect participation in the Gov-ernment." Provisions of this kind had been lacking in the con-stitutions in his *West African Countries*, which emphasized the duties of the rulers rather than the rights of the ruled. Co-operation with the British government would be secured by constituting the administrator "Protector" of the Confederation, and by giving the president a seat on the Colony's Legislative Council.

The letters were published in London by W. J. Johnson in 1870. The Colonial Office made no objection to publication. On the title page his name appeared as "Africanus B. Horton," with the titles of his previous publications, his honours, and his qual-ifications. He added a preface, making again the point he had made in *West African Countries,* that Africa, like Britain and Germany in the days of the Roman Empire, was now emerging from barbarism—and was plainly emerging more rapidly than they had done. He included the text of the Anglo-Dutch treaty of 1867, and a dedication to Kennedy.

He had had to pay for the publication of his previous books himself. To finance the *Letters,* which were intended for private circulation, he invited subscriptions. The subscribers from Cape Coast alone provided £30, enough to pay for the book. They

16. Ibid. 151-58.

consisted chiefly of members of the mercantile community, African and European, with a few colonial and military officials; the colonial government contributed five guineas.

Until the *Letters* appeared Horton was on good terms with Administrator Ussher, who subscribed for the book, corresponded amicably over his educational plans, and appointed him to act as Colonial Surgeon during a temporary vacancy.[17] But with publication his feelings changed. It may have been, as was suggested at the Colonial Office, that he took offence at Horton's asking Lord Granville to appoint only tactful, conciliatory administrators—suspecting, no doubt correctly, that this was implied criticism of him.

Whatever may have motivated it, he sent off to Kennedy in January 1871 a most virulent attack on Horton. He accused him of associating with the Fanti Confederation, which he persistently regarded as a dangerous organization, and of collecting debts owed to Fitzgerald for the *African Times*. Though obliged to admit, "I am not in a position to accuse Dr Horton of overt acts," he proposed to remove him from the bench of magistrates, and asked to have him sent away to another colony.

He found an ally in Horton's medical superior, Staff-Surgeon Mosse, who, like O'Callaghan in 1861, was only too ready to asperse his African colleague. Mosse had already reported him to London for writing a letter, which he thought objectionable, to a Cape Coast newspaper. He now forwarded a copy of Ussher's unsubstantiated complaints.

Kennedy was annoyed and embarrassed by this unsubstantiated vilification of a man who had praised him so generously in print —particularly as Ussher, never noted for tact, had suggested that he was under Horton's influence. Regulations required him to forward the letter to London, but he added a despatch of his own, deploring Ussher's violent tone and defending Horton. "Dr Horton is a pure native" (by that he meant that he was not a mulatto, which would have made him immediately suspect), "and I have never heard a word to his detriment either in his private or professional capacity."

17. P.R.O., C.O. 96/85, Kennedy, 61, May 11, 1870, enclosure.

At the Colonial Office they supported Kennedy, as they usually did, and found no grounds for censuring Horton. It was pointed out that the Fanti Confederation was only endeavouring to carry out the 1865 policy, and that Horton was perfectly justified in supporting it. Ussher was in any case known to be hasty and indiscreet. The Director-General of the Army Medical Department (to whom Horton had dedicated his *Guinea Worm*) was also sympathetic: "I know Dr Horton to be a good Medical Officer, never to have been otherwise than amenable to discipline."[18]

Meanwhile the members of the Fanti Confederation followed Horton's advice and drew up a formal constitution. It provided for a National Assembly of kings and chiefs, to meet annually and elect a king-president who would rule with an executive council of elected and appointed ministers. Each king and chief was to nominate two representatives—one a chief, the other educated—to a Representative Assembly, or legislature. Provision was made for administration, fiscal arrangements, and relations with the British government. Their general policy statement included among its aims the development of education and of economic resources.

This constitution gave more power to the traditional rulers than Horton had proposed. There was no popular representation, no statement of citizens' rights. But in a society where traditional hierarchies were still so entrenched, it provided a more immediately acceptable and realistic formula. Above all, it specificially looked forward to what Horton believed to be the prerequisite of any African constitution—educational and economic development.

The first National Assembly meeting revealed an inner weakness, conflicts between individuals, that Horton, like many constitution-makers, had tended to overlook. Two rival kings contested for the king-presidency, and had eventually to be appointed to rule jointly. Ghartey was relegated to membership of the Executive Council. Other educated Fanti were elected ministers. Fitzgerald was appointed agent in England. He publi-

18. P.R.O., C.O. 96/87, Kennedy, May 26, 1871, with minutes and enclosures.

cized their proceedings in the *African Times,* heralding "the birth of a NATION," and began sending letters on their behalf to the Colonial Office.[19]

Ussher went to England in July 1871, leaving Charles Salmon, the Colonial Secretary, to act as administrator. Salmon had originally gone out from England to Sierra Leone in 1861, at a period of bitter colour strife in Freetown. The governor, Colonel Hill, was conducting a feud against the senior law officer, Alexander Fitzjames, an Afro-West Indian, accusing him of stirring up a mulatto conspiracy. Salmon ingratiated himself with the governor by reporting a private conversation which he said he had overheard. As a result, Hill's opponent was dismissed, and Salmon was rewarded with an official post.[20] Eventually he was promoted to the Gold Coast. By the standards of the service he was a competent officer, but at the Colonial Office they thought him "not quite gentleman enough" to be made permanently administrator.[21]

When Salmon was sent a copy of the Fanti Confederation's constitution he reacted even more violently than Ussher. Resenting any apparent threat to his brief authority, he immediately had the members of the Fanti Executive Council arrested. He sent off the news to Freetown with despatches alleging that the Confederation was a dangerous conspiracy, stirred up by the educated members, whose real motive was to enrich themselves by levying taxes on the Fanti people.

Kennedy had now lost interest in Africa; he was shortly to leave it, to govern Hong Kong. He had become obsessed with his feud against Rainy and Fitzgerald. As the latter was agent for the Confederation, and the former came into his detested category of "mulatto," he took Salmon's wild outpourings as ammunition against them. He gave his approval to the arrests, and wrote to the Colonial Office, "I am informed and believe that the 'Constitution' was drawn by Messrs Fitzgerald and Rainy." He added that the promoters of the Confederation were "for the

---

19. Fitzgerald's letters are in P.R.O., C.O. 96/95.
20. For this episode see Christopher Fyfe, *A History of Sierra Leone* (London, 1962), 313-15.
21. P.R.O., C.O. 87/102, Hennessy, 52, Oct. 9, 1872, minute.

most part mulattoes who having failed in all honest business have now as a last resource adopted Patriotism."[22]

But at the Colonial Office Salmon's highhanded violence roused alarm. Again it was pointed out that the Confederation, far from being an illegal conspiracy, was a logical fulfillment of the 1865 policy. Even Kennedy when he arrived back in the temperate London air, admitted that the arrests had been unwarrantable. Salmon was ordered to release the prisoners, whom he had already let out on bail. Nevertheless, he was told to issue a proclamation warning British subjects against joining the Confederation—which seemed to imply official disapproval of it.

In his despatches Salmon had smeared all the leading educated Fanti as drunken, immoral, dishonest and, if possible, mulattos. J. H. Brew, whose great-grandfather had been an Irishman, he called "a penniless lawyer, with an *awful* private character (a half caste)." Nor was Horton forgotten. Though Salmon had to admit that he had no evidence to connect him directly with the constitution-makers, "the opinion is universal, especially with his own countrymen, that he has been a principal adviser."[23] Solemnly he declared, "There is a man here who is glad to keep the Confederation afloat he hopes ultimately to be *king* (Horton)."[24] Neither Kennedy nor the Colonial Office reacted on paper to these assertions. Nor was official notice taken of a subsequent report by Ussher on his return from leave asserting, again without evidence, that Horton and Fitzgerald had masterminded the whole movement.

Amid the political turmoil, a severe smallpox epidemic broke out in December 1871 round Mumford, east of Cape Coast. The Civil Commandant Major Brownwell, Horton's old antagonist, reported that the people refused vaccination, and stayed at home, burying the dead in their houses and spreading infection. Horton hurried to help. Together they forced the patients to move to a new site, and spent a hot Christmas Day burning down the infected houses. Brownwell then departed, leaving Horton to vac-

22. P.R.O., C.O. 96/89, Kennedy, 152, Dec. 16, 1871, with minutes and enclosures; C.O. 96/92, Kennedy, Feb. 1, 1872.
23. P.R.O., C.O. 96/92, Kennedy, Jan. 3, 1872.
24. P.R.O., C.O. 96/89, Kennedy, 152, Dec. 16, 1871, enclosures.

cinate the people. With the despotic benevolence he always favoured, he decided to start with the two senior chiefs. They
declined, alleging their bowels were out of order. Without further argument he marched them off to the market place and
vaccinated them there publicly. After that the people came
crowding in for vaccination.

An account of his exertions was sent to the Colonial Office
and greatly impressed the officials. As it was not part of an army
doctor's regular duties to cope with epidemics among the civilian
population, he was officially thanked and given a present of £50,
which Lord Kimberley, the Secretary of State minuted "he well
deserves."[25] Subsequently he claimed, and was paid, an additional £200, on the basis of one shilling for each successful vaccination.[26]

THE CONFEDERATION IN DECLINE

As Kennedy left abruptly for Hong Kong, a successor was ur-
gently needed to go and take formal possession of the ceded
Dutch forts. John Pope Hennessy, already appointed Governor
of the Bahamas, was sent out temporarily to do so. Hennessy always constituted himself the champion of disfavoured groups in
the many territories he successively governed. He therefore
showed sympathy with the Fanti Confederation and repudiated
Ussher's policy. At his request its leaders gave him a policy statement, with a budget drawn up on lines Horton would have approved. Out of £20,040 estimated expenditure, £4000 was allocated for education, £4000 for roads, and £2000 for medical
services. It was another eighty years or so before the items in a
West African budget were again allocated with such priorities.

Nevertheless, Hennessy would not champion the Confederation
with more than fine words. He refused to recommend its policy
to the Colonial Office. Instead he recommended "a firm extension of Her Majesty's authority" over the whole coastal area,
which should be ruled as a colony.[27] In London the officials were

25. P.R.O., C.O. 96/92, Kennedy, 5, Jan. 3, 1872; Kennedy, 13, Jan. 9, 1872;
Hennessy, 32, Mar. 16, 1872, and minutes and enclosures.
26. P.R.O., C.O. 96/111, Wolseley, 63, Mar. 2, 1874.
27. P.R.O., C.O. 96/94, Hennessy, 93, Oct. 29, 1872, with enclosures; the quoted
passage is on fol. 135.

ready enough to shelve the 1865 policy, but not to take on new responsibilities. Instead, Lord Kimberley was able (in David Kimble's words) "to offer some cogent reasons for doing nothing." But he wanted to hear no more of the Confederation, or of what he elsewhere described as "the so-called educated Negro." He wrote firmly, "I would have nothing to do with the 'educated natives' as a body. I would treat with the hereditary Chiefs only, and endeavour as far as possible to govern through them."[28]

The Confederation had, in any case, lost its impetus. Taxes could no longer be raised: by 1871 it was being financed by Richard Ghartey's firm. The educated Fanti, closely linked to the British towns where most of them gained their livelihood, were unwilling to go on being associated with an organization which the British government repudiated. Their first objective, expelling the Dutch, had been easily achieved. The second, taking over from the British, was further off than ever, when even their ostensible well-wisher Hennessy could completely ignore the principles of the 1865 resolutions. Horton's dream of "Self-Government for the Gold Coast," which had seemed to be on the verge of realization in 1870, was rapidly fading.

HORTON AND THE COLONIAL OFFICE

Horton welcomed Hennessy's conciliatory ways. He did not know that the governor was recommending in his despatches to the Colonial Office a policy that meant death to the Fanti Confederation. Hennessy in return thought well of him, and sent him to act as Civil Commandant at Sekondi, west of Elmina. This appointment, which included responsibility for the local customs posts as well as magistrate's duties, gave him an extra £250 a year; in addition he received £60 as a civil medical officer.

His work there included reconciling the coastal peoples with their neighbours inland, and reopening the trade routes to the interior, which had been closed during the last years of the Dutch presence. The sycophantic Charles Salmon who had defamed him to Kennedy, now praised him to Hennessy, with whom he had managed to ingratiate himself.[29] Hennessy passed

28. David Kimble, *A Political History of Ghana* (Oxford, 1963), 259-60.
29. P.R.O., C.O. 96/114, Salmon, May 6, 1874, minute.

on Salmon's report to the Colonial Office, adding his own com-
mendation of Horton's "zeal and intelligence." Kimberley minuted, "Dr Horton seems to be a useful man."[30]

Hennessy recommended him for head of the government medical department in Sierra Leone. A doctor of part-African descent,
Dr. Robert Smith, was already acting in this vacant post, but
though he was a good doctor he was never promoted substantively. At the Colonial Office it was thought desirable to have a
white doctor in charge. This also excluded Horton, who was
"perfectly black."[31] Though officials might believe that a "pure
black" (in Kennedy's words) was "better in every way than a
mixed breed,"[32] he could still not be allowed to rank over a pure
white.

This he did not yet realize. In 1872 Ussher was invalided and
Horton applied to the Colonial Office for the vacant post of administrator of the Gold Coast. Under regulations, his application
had to be sent through the governor-in-chief, and by the time it
reached Freetown a successor, Colonel Harley, had already been
appointed. Nevertheless, Hennessy sent the letter in which he
had detailed his services and achievements to London, adding a
note of "the high opinion I entertain of Dr Horton's ability and
zeal. Indeed I regard him as one of the most useful officers on the
Coast of Africa."

Horton wrote to Kimberley—

My Lord

The Administratorship of the Government of the Gold Coast having
become vacant by the retirement of H. J. Ussher Esquire from the
Coast, I have the honour most respectfully to tender herewith an
application for the vacant post.

I have served for nearly fourteen years on the West Coast of Africa
in the Medical Department of the Imperial Service, where several
times I have been placed in positions of great responsibility and having
junior European Medical Officers under me. I have held offices in
every branch of the Military Department on this Coast; thus I have
several times been Military Commandant, commanding Detachments
in important military posts;—Acting Deputy Assistant Commissariat

30. P.R.O., C.O. 96/93, Hennessy, 81, Sept. 28, 1872, and minute.
31. P.R.O., C.O. 267/316, Hennessy, 87, July 29, 1872, and minutes.
32. P.R.O., C.O. 267/314, Rainy, Oct. 18, 1871, minute.

General and Acting Assistant Commissary in large stations, and being the sole officer of that department in one of these stations viz. Lagos, had large sums of money passed through my hands; I have also been both acting Barrack Master and acting Superintendent of Stores.

I have held several colonial appointments of great trust, requiring sound judgment and political common sense, and have filled these offices to the expressed satisfaction of the superior officers of the Government. I have several times held the post of Civil Commandant both on the Gold Coast and at the Gambia and often when difficult cases were pending received letters from the Chief Executive of the confidence the Government had in my ability and judgment. I have held for several years the Commission of Justice of the Peace, and have had important missions committed to my trust by the Colonial Government of the Coast, in one of which the Chief Executive, in forwarding a general report of the mission to the Governor-in-Chief, wrote to me to say, that he was going to forward copies of my report on the subject "in order that the highest authorities may judge for themselves of the arduous nature of the duty I undertook and the very efficient manner in which I performed it," and that he was convinced that were it not for the energy, perseverance and patience I brought to bear with tact upon the performance of the mission "we would have had to lament a loss of life fearful to contemplate."[33] His Excellency the Administrator-in-Chief in forwarding to me a handsome gratuity from Her Majesty's Principal Secretary of State for the Colonies conveyed also Your Lordship's "warm thanks for the zeal, courage and energy with which I performed" that duty.

I have made, the proper government of the West Coast of Africa, a subject of close and practical study, and I fully endorse the policy so ably carried out with telling effect by His Excellency Governor Pope Hennessy, Administrator-in-Chief of Her Majesty's West African Settlements viz. that of peace, conciliation and goodwill amongst Her Majesty's subjects.

That my studies and observations might be of advantage, I have published at considerable expense, the following works on the West Coast of Africa:—

1. Physical and Medical Climate and Meteorology of the West Coast of Africa, with valuable hints to Europeans for the preservation of health in the tropics.

2. Political Economy of British West Africa, with the Requirements of the several colonies and settlements.

3. West African Countries and Peoples . . .

4. Letters on the Political Condition of the Gold Coast . . .

I have published other works and papers bearing on subjects connected with this Coast and have always argued that by adopting

33. That is, his work during the smallpox epidemic at Mumford.

conciliatory measures and courteous behaviour to the natives, the country will always be in a prosperous and peaceable state.

I cannot close, My Lord, without expressing the deep sense of gratitude the inhabitants of the West Coast of Africa owe to Her Majesty's Government for the warm interest it has always shown towards their advancement.

I have the honor to be
Your Lordship's Most Obedient Humble Servant
J. A. B. Horton M.D.
Army Medical Staff.

His previous relations with the Colonial Office had been friendly. His letters had been received with interest; he had been exonerated from the charges brought by Ussher and Salmon; he had been given a present for his exertions during the small-pox epidemic. Kimberley had commented on him favourably. But whatever his abilities, his colour was against him. "Dr Africanus Horton (a pure black) is, I believe, a good medical officer," minuted Kimberley's private secretary, "but I don't think it would do to make an Administrator of him." The adulatory passage about Hennessy did him no good: Hennessy was no longer approved of at the Colonial Office. Nor did his recital of his own achievements—though it was no more self-congratulatory than what was regularly received from applicants for official posts. "Dr Horton . . . doubtless possesses some of the numerous attributes with which he credits himself," was the only comment.

Kimberley had previously been Viceroy of Ireland, where he had become accustomed to formulate policies in racial terms. "The true source of Irish unhappiness," he noted in his diary, "is the character of the Irish race."[34] In any racial hierarchy Africans were bound to rank even lower. "A jury of Englishmen," he once wrote, "is a tolerable institution—a jury of Irishmen often intolerable—a jury of blacks I should say always intolerable." His verdict on Horton was abrupt. "Dr Africanus Horton's letter is quite sufficient to prove that he is unfit for an administrative appointment."[35]

34. Ethel Drus (ed.), *A Journal of Events by John, First Earl of Kimberley* (London, 1958), 9-10.
35. P.R.O., C.O. 96/94, Hennessy, 90, Oct. 24, 1872, with enclosure and minutes.

COMMANDANT AT SEKONDI

Sekondi, where Horton was in charge as Civil Commandant, was an uneasy station. Formerly there had been British and Dutch forts there, side by side, each with its own dependent town under its own king. The two towns were in long-standing hostility. When the British authorities moved out in 1868 and handed over to the Dutch, the king of the "British" town, Kobina Inkatier, moved out, too, and established himself inland. From there he carried on intermittent warfare against his uncle, the king of the "Dutch" town, Kwamina Andries, and prevented traders from coming down to the coast.

In 1872 the Dutch departed. Hennessy visited Sekondi to try and persuade Andries to let the "British" party return. A young British officer was left as commandant to reconcile them. But though Andries was friendly to Hennessy he had no intention of letting his nephew return. He besieged the commandant in the dilapidated old Dutch fort, a semi-ruin with no proper water supply, defying him to come out and remove the Dutch flag which he had hoisted again. After this humiliation the commandant was recalled, and Horton was sent to replace him.

Patiently and tactfully he began persuading Andries to allow his nephew back. Within four months he had won him round. Inkatier and his people were welcomed back to Sekondi, as Horton described it, "under a tremendous fire of musketry with blank ammunition accompanied by great dancing and rejoicings and presents from the Dutch kings and chiefs to the new arrivals."[36]

The two kings assented to a constitutional agreement he drew up for them, assigning each his respective spheres of government. Trade revived; ostensibly the country seemed to be at peace again. But they still remained hostile. Old disputes soon revived. Vainly he tried to reconcile them. In January 1873 he summoned them to the fort to settle their differences. They arrived drunk and soon came to blows. He ordered them out,

36. P.R.O., C.O. 96/93, Hennessy, 81, Sept. 28, 1872; C.O. 96/114, Horton, June 4, 1874.

keeping Inkatier back for a while to give him a special caution to preserve the peace. Later, hearing that trouble was starting in the near by villages, he spent all evening till one o'clock trying unsuccessfully to calm the townspeople.

Next morning he sat down and wrote two reports on his proceedings for the administrator, Colonel Harley. At ten o'clock he had finished, and was taking a bath, when he heard firing. Andries with seven or eight hundred men was attacking Inkatier's town, burning it down, with some loss of life, and looting the store of a British firm. Horton had only a corporal and nineteen soldiers, with a West Indian sergeant, Robert Brown, who had arrived two days earlier with the soldiers' pay. Horton, like his predecessor, knew he could not defend the rotten old fort. He issued arms to his tiny garrison, but dared not risk leading them out against such heavy odds into the narrow lanes that clustered round the fort, where they could easily be surrounded and killed.[37]

"Can't you march us down and see if we can't pacify them?" asked Sergeant Brown.

"No, my good man," Horton replied, "I can't march you down amongst them, the houses are very thick, and some of you may get shot, and I will have to answer for it."[38]

Instead he tried firing rockets over the town to stop the fighting, but without success (as he noted in a third report). Eventually Inkatier hoisted a white flag. Horton sent three of his policemen and the jailer to negotiate. Andries agreed and the fighting stopped. Horton persuaded him to withdraw from Inkatier's smouldering town, and then sat down to write a further report (his fourth that day) to Colonel Harley, to the sound of drumming, dancing, and firing off guns by the victorious party.

Next day all was quiet. People who had hurried in from neighbouring towns to join in the fighting were told it was over; they were given a drink of rum and sent home. Horton went out to inspect the damage, and sent messengers to "beat gong gong" through the neighbouring villages, announcing peace. The day after, a naval cruiser arrived, bringing the Inspector-General of Police, Colonel Foster, from Cape Coast. He and Horton arrested

37. P.R.O., C.O. 96/96, Keate, 8, Mar. 1, 1873, enclosures.
38. P.R.O., C.O. 96/96, Keate, 1, Feb. 21, 1873, enclosure.

the two kings and their principal chiefs. They were sent to Elmina and kept in prison for some months; Andries was eventually deported to Sierra Leone.[39]

Harley, in Cape Coast, and Hennessy, in Freetown, hated one
another. Harley therefore used the Sekondi riot as a means of
discrediting Hennessy and his African protégé. He had never
met Horton, but may well have known about, and perhaps resented, his having applied for the administratorship. Whatever
his motives, his behaviour was unquestionably vindictive.

When Sergeant Brown got back to headquarters he made a
sworn statement before two of his officers (Horton's comrades-in-
arms) suggesting that Horton had neglected his duty by remaining in the fort instead of coming out to attack. Harley at once
wrote to the commanding officer asking to have a regimental
officer put over Horton at Sekondi, and suggesting that there
had been negligence—although he had not yet received any detailed report from him or from Colonel Foster. Only four days
later, when he knew that news of the episode would already have
reached army headquarters in Freetown, did he write to Hennessy, blaming Horton, and promising to give fuller details later.
Hennessy was obliged to forward the despatch with its one-sided
accusations to London. Kimberley commented, "Dr Horton is I
suppose Dr 'Africanus' Horton, and I am not surprised that he
had not influence enough to stop this unlucky quarrel. I fear
except in quite subordinate posts we cannot safely employ natives."

Hennessy replied to Harley that Horton had "hitherto shown
himself to be one of the best officers in Her Majesty's Service
on the Gold Coast," and that he was not prepared to accept an
unsupported opinion to the contrary. To be revenged, he instructed Harley to ask the members of his Legislative Council
to give him their opinions on the Sekondi riot in writing and
send them to Freetown—a clear way of indicating that Harley's
own opinions were not to be trusted.[40]

Horton, meanwhile, had been making a statement in his own
defence. When the three Legislative Council members read it,
the two official members, who included Foster, were immediately

39. P.R.O., C.O. 96/101, Harley, 203, Aug. 23, 1873.
40. P.R.O., C.O. 96/96, Hennessy, 13, Feb. 2, 1873; Hennessy, 19, Feb. 8, 1873.

convinced that he had acted properly in not risking his men's lives. Nothing, Foster declared, "could be more hazardous than to march a small body of men between these contending parties. . . . I am of opinion that Dr Horton acted with prudence." The third Council member, Horton's old friend George Blankson, contented himself with saying that as he was neither a soldier nor a lawyer he could express no opinion.

Unsupported by his Council, Harley nevertheless still insisted that Horton was blameworthy. "I am informed," he wrote, "that Dr Horton never left the fort, nor did he interfere in any way to suppress the rioting." As Hennessy had by now left Africa, he wrote to the new governor asking for Horton not to be restored in charge of Sekondi.

But the governor, confronted with the Council's views and Horton's own explanation, saw no reason for censure. At the Colonial Office, too, it was now felt that he had shown prudence and common sense. Even Kimberley agreed, and instructed Harley that if Horton were to be superseded at Sekondi, he must be clearly informed that it was not for any negligence during the riots.[41]

Davidson Nicol, a Sierra Leone doctor who, like Horton, has distinguished himself in research, literature, and administration, has seen the story of the Sekondi riot not merely in terms of Horton's own personal dilemma, but in the wider context of Africa in the decolonization era—an era which Horton dreamed of but never lived to see.

> As we lean over Horton's shoulder at his desk in the beleaguered fort, watching him writing or dictating his despatches with the sound of shouting and gunfire around, and the cries nearby of his compatriots slaying each other, we are not simply watching a ghost of the distant past. We are witnessing the tests and trials of self-government in the first of the many thousands of Africans young and old who now hold positions of lonely responsibility in their own countries, surrounded always by a critical audience—sometimes of their own people[42]

41. P.R.O., C.O. 96/96, Keate, 8, Mar. 1, 1873, with enclosures, minutes, and draft despatch.
42. Davidson Nicol, *Africanus Horton* (London, 1969), 79-80.

THE ANGLO–ASHANTI WAR OF 1873–74

The Ashanti were closely affected by the political changes on the coast. They had been inclined to welcome the Anglo-Dutch partition treaty of 1867 which gave them, through their Dutch allies, a wider sphere of potential influence. But they did not welcome the Fanti Confederation—the sudden alarming fusion of their long-divided enemies into a powerful organization. Above all, the Dutch cession of Elmina was an open insult to Ashanti sovereignty. For the Dutch authorities, as holders of the "note" for Elmina, were still making payments to the Asantahene, and whatever they might maintain to the contrary, he considered that these payments were rent, exacted from a tenant.

A new Asantahene, Kofi Kakari, was installed in 1869, "a fiery young man of thirty-five," according to Horton[43] (who, aged thirty-four himself, still considered thirty-five "young"). However, he dissembled for a while, even apparently assenting to a document in which he renounced his claim to Elmina. But unobtrusively he was preparing war, and early in 1873 his armies crossed the Pra to get back what he considered his own territory.

The Colony government was taken by surprise. As usual, no attempt was made to protect the "Protectorate," and the Ashanti armies swept down to the outskirts of Cape Coast and Elmina, scattering Fanti resistance.

Horton, at Sekondi, had only seventeen policemen to defend a large district where many of the inhabitants were traditionally associated with the Dutch and sympathized with the Ashanti. Soon they began retaliating on those who were associated with the British. He managed to prevent open warfare, and rescued some people who had been seized as slaves. Then he was recalled to army headquarters for other duties. At once the district was in an uproar which his successor, a regimental officer, was unable to cope with.

Two small fortified camps were hastily built, one near Elmina, the other near Cape Coast, for defence against the besieging

43. Horton, *Letters*, 84.

Ashanti. They were garrisoned by Fanti volunteers and by Hausa police, recruited in Lagos. In August, with the rainy season still on, a detachment of the 2nd West India Regiment took over. Horton accompanied them as medical officer. At "Napoleon" camp, near Cape Coast, he was taken seriously ill with bronchitis, the effect of exposure to the wet, and had to be invalided for six months.[44]

Elmina was the principal Ashanti objective. But with naval reinforcement from the sea the defenders were able to hold out. After a sharp repulse in June, the Ashanti offensive subsided, and as the year wore on the armies retired across the Pra. They had failed in their principal objective, but had waged another successful punitive expedition (as in 1863–64) against the Fanti and the British.

The British government, however, was not this time prepared to give up so easily. Colonel Harley, who had spent most of the summer quarrelling with his colleagues, was superseded. Major-General Sir Garnet Wolseley, one of the popular military heroes of the late Victorian era, who had already gained fame from campaigns in India and Canada, was sent to replace him. But memories of the disastrous 1863–64 war still held the government back. Wolseley was not allowed to take out white soldiers to fight and die in the bush, only a cadre of white officers, who were to recruit African troops.

But the Fanti were uninterested in fighting for Wolseley. Their own organization, the Fanti Confederation, had been broken. The Ashanti were withdrawing, and they saw no need to pursue them. They knew the British were faithless allies—and could evaluate Wolseley's talk about bringing them "civilization" in terms of what British influence had in fact meant to them over the preceding decades. Nor was Wolseley sorry. He was determined to fight with white troops. Even the West India Regiments he despised—and backed up his low opinion of them with evidence supplied him by Horton's old persecutor, Colonel (as he now was) de Ruvignes.[45] Before he had even reached Cape

44. P.R.O., C.O. 96/102, Harley, 235, Sept. 13, 1873; C.O. 96/114, Horton, June 4, 1874.
45. P.R.O., C.O. 96/107, War Office, Nov. 24, 1873, enclosure by Wolseley.

Coast he was writing to his wife, "the Africans are like so many monkeys; they are a good-for-nothing race."[46]

The government had therefore to relent and send him white troops. They arrived in December, marched rapidly inland, captured and destroyed Kumasi, and returned home as quickly as possible. The Asantahene retreated as they advanced, and was not strictly defeated in battle. Nevertheless, it was a severe blow to Ashanti prestige. As the white troops hurried back from the front, detachments of the West India Regiments (who had not been allowed to go to Kumasi) replaced them, to carry out an orderly withdrawal. Horton, who had now rejoined them, even though not fully recovered, was in medical charge.

All Wolseley's efforts had gone into caring for his own soldiers' health. During their brief campaign they had enjoyed a standard of comfort never seen in the British army before: "each camp was like a hotel," a newspaper reporter commented.[47] The West India Regiments he treated as a transport corps, to carry supplies, and once his white troops had gone he took little further interest in them. In their makeshift quarters on the Pra it was the story of 1863–64 over again. Out of one detachment of 200 men Horton had 103 in hospital with fever, dysentery, and liver complaints.[48] At last, in April 1874, he accompanied the last of the sickly units back to the coast. As a correspondent for the *African Times* commented, he had "led the van of the army and brought back the rear."[49]

Wolseley's Ashanti War can be seen as a rehearsal for the wars of the subsequent European Scramble for Africa. It proved what had been in doubt—that white soldiers could campaign successfully in the African bush. Moreover it was publicized as no previous colonial war had ever been. Newspaper correspondents flocked in, with Wolseley's active encouragement, including two noted "African explorers"—Winwood Reade for the London

46. Quoted in W. D. McIntyre, "British Policy in West Africa: The Ashanti Expedition of 1873–74," in *Historical Journal*, vol. v, no. 1 (1962), 37.
47. Winwood Reade, *The Story of the Ashantee Campaign* (London, 1874), 268.
48. Horton, *Diseases*, pp. viii, 22; P.R.O., C.O. 96/111, Johnston, 99, April 20, 1874.
49. *African Times*, May 30, 1874.

Times, and the much more famous Henry M. Stanley for the *New York Herald*. Wolseley and his officers, many of whom were members of the English nobility, were built up as heroes, and the public was given a foretaste of the kind of emotive journalism, appealing strongly to feelings of racial pride and racial domination, which was to accompany the white man's march over Africa.

This publicity build-up rankled bitterly in the West India Regiments. Medals (including no less than five Victoria Crosses), decorations, and promotions were handed out generously to Wolseley's officers, while they were forgotten. Horton felt particularly embittered that his services during 1873 and 1874—for the colonial government at Sekondi, for the military at the Pra—received no recognition at all. He wrote angrily to the Colonial Office, complaining that his successor at Sekondi (who had failed to cope with the disorders he had managed to check) had been promoted, and that while "honours and awards are being showered" on Wolseley's officers, "I who have had a good deal of the anxieties, toils and real hard work have not had the slightest recognition of Service."

At the Colonial Office they felt some sympathy for him. He was sent a letter of approbation (with, however, a prim reminder that not everyone can be specially rewarded for their services), and a copy was sent to the War Office for inclusion in his records, and another to the governor as a public notification of his services.[50] Otherwise, apart from the award of the general Ashanti War medal, he remained unrecognized.

The war brought a change in British policy. In 1874 the cumbrous West African Settlements were broken up. The Gold Coast Colony, with Lagos attached until 1886, was constituted a separate government and given responsibility for the Protectorate. Though the extent of the responsibility was still not defined, the coastal rulers were plainly no longer sovereign. British sovereignty was there to stay. The policy of the 1865 resolutions had been quietly abandoned—and with it Horton's dream of establishing self-government.

50. **P.R.O.**, C.O. 96/114, Horton, June 4, 1874; C.O. 96/113, War Office, July 25, 1874.

VI

DREAMS OF DEVELOPMENT

DISEASES OF TROPICAL CLIMATES

Now THAT THERE WAS NO further prospect of immediate self-government for British West Africa, Horton returned to medicine and geology. He published no more political books. His next publication was his long-planned *Diseases of Tropical Climates*. Then, for the remainder of his years in the service, he devoted himself increasingly to schemes for developing the mineral resources of West Africa. Thwarted in his quest for political development, he turned instead to the economic development that he believed must accompany it.

In 1859, in the Preface to his *Medical Topography*, he had impetuously announced the forthcoming appearance of a book on tropical diseases. Wisely, he postponed production until he had gained more experience. By 1873 it was in proof stage: he revised the proofs "while busily engaged in the field in the recent Ashantee Campaign." The Preface was dated October 1874, and Churchill published it in that year.

The Diseases of Tropical Climates and Their Treatment was longer than his earlier books and its scope wider. He included all tropical countries, not just West Africa (though, as a reviewer pointed out, the Indian coverage was inevitably perfunctory).[1]

---

1. *Medical Press and Circular,* Jan. 27, 1875 (quoted in *Independent,* May 27, 1875); another reviewer suggested he might have done better to confine the book to his own personal experience (*Medical Times and Gazette,* June 14, 1879).

It was intended primarily as a reference book for the medical profession. His aim was "placing in the hands of young practitioners, a handbook of practical importance and utility in their early career." Systematically he brought together the material available on diseases prevalent in the tropics, drawing as usual on a wide range of reading. His authorities again included Sir Ranald Martin, to whom he dedicated the book—though, as before, he was ready to criticize him when they disagreed. He added observations and comments based on his own years of research and practice, including formulae for medicines, nearly all of which he had used himself. It was, therefore, much more than a mere compilation.

Plainly, there was a demand for such a book, as pre-publication subscriptions nearly covered the cost of production. It was favourably reviewed, and a revised edition appeared in 1879.[2] Though the format and price of the second edition were the same as the first, the type was completely reset, and small changes were made throughout the text. Some were stylistic (rephrasing or correcting errors that had escaped his eye on the banks of the Pra), some incorporated new material he had read or observed since 1874. With these additions the second edition had 696 pages (the first had 669).

In the presentation of this book (and in his two contributions to the Army Medical Department Annual Reports) there was one striking difference from his previous publications. On the title page he followed the style used by most British contemporaries and described himself with his initials, as "J. A. B. Horton." This was how he signed official letters; his visiting card, too, read "Dr J. A. B. Horton."[3] Nowhere in the book does the name "Africanus" or the description "Native of Sierra Leone" appear. Indeed, one reviewer seems to have supposed that he was an Englishman who had served abroad—"in all, he has spent fifteen years in the tropics."

2. Two reviews from English journals were reprinted in the Freetown *Independent,* May 27, Aug. 12, 1875; others appeared in *The British Mail,* Nov. 3, 1875, and *Medical Times and Gazette,* June 14, 1879.
3. One of his visiting cards survives in the MS Collection of the Royal Geographical Society, London, pinned onto a memo from Messrs Radcliffe & Durant of Liverpool, dated July 31, 1876, asking for the back numbers of the Society's journals to be forwarded to him at Cape Coast.

The book is divided into three long sections—fevers, abdominal diseases, and other tropical diseases. In each section there is a breakdown into subsections for each specific disease, with a detailed account of its symptoms, causes, and treatment.

As always, he was quick to notice correlations with climate and soil. In the second edition he suggested a possible correlation between the phases of malaria and the phases of the moon.[4] As in his *Physical and Medical Climate,* he called attention to the salutary effects of ozone, deduced from "experiments made on myself and officers serving with me."[5] He recommended quinine as an anti-malarial prophylactic (it had been generally used since Baikie's experiment in 1854), and in the second edition noted that it was now manufactured in pill form. If quinine was not available, he suggested instead a remedy used by a doctor in India—pills made out of spiders' webs.

> I have tried this remedy while serving with the troops in Western Africa during the commencement of the rainy season, and although the number treated was not such (being ten) as to warrant the establishment of an opinion, yet still I might state that in every case the most satisfactory results were obtained.[6]

He still had to caution against injudicious use of mercury, and even against indiscriminate blood-letting, an eighteenth-century remedy that was apparently in use in the 1870's.

He brought overwhelming evidence, from his own experience with the West India Regiments and in treating Africans, against the theory, which was still maintained, that people of African descent were immune to malaria. His own case history would have been equally conclusive. Later in the book he noted that he had found splenitis most prevalent "among the offspring of white and black parents, or that of two mulattoes."[7] But nowhere else did he mention race as a determinant, or non-determinant, of disease; nor did he consider racial theories.

As well as recommending medicines which the practitioner was to make up from formula, he included a long paragraph in

4. Horton, *Diseases* (2nd ed.), 79.
5. Horton, *Diseases,* 49-50.
6. Ibid. 44.
7. Ibid. 480.

praise of a much-used anti-malarial patent medicine, Lam-plough's Pyretic Saline, "which should be possessed by every family residing in the tropics."[8] His friend Fitzgerald, who had great faith in it, was able to quote this favourable opinion in the *African Times.*

The section on abdominal diseases, over half the book, in-cluded diseases of the liver and spleen, as well as dyspepsia, dys-entery, and cholera. His account of dysentery was illustrated from his experiences at the Pra camp in 1864. Cholera, which he had witnessed in the Gambia in 1869, he believed to be depend-ent, like malaria, "on some atmospheric miasmatic exhalation."[9] He noted with surprise that, though most liver complaints among Europeans in the tropics were caused by heavy drinking, he had nevertheless only found jaundice in patients who lived temperately.[10]

The third section grouped together a variety of other maladies, including anaemia, beri-beri (which he related to soil conditions), *delirium tremens,* sunstroke, goitre, and yaws. The description of the guinea worm, taken substantially from his previous pub-lications, added an inconclusive experiment he had recently made to trace the phases of the worm's life outside the human body. He described a native African method of treating yaws, and another for curing excessive drinkers (a pragmatic example of aversion therapy):

> Soak fresh beef secretly in the liquor the drunkard delights in, and when it is taken, it produces severe nausea and vomiting, and a general distaste for any spirituous liquors.[11]

Earlier in the book he had mentioned treatment of dysentery with locally gathered astringent barks. Otherwise his medicine was based on European methods: he omitted boa-constrictor fat as a cure for rheumatism, "used by the natives of the Bight of Benin," which he had included in his *Physical and Medical Cli-mate.*

In an appendix he repeated the hints to Europeans that he had

8. Ibid. 38.
9. Ibid. 290.
10. Horton, *Diseases* (2nd ed.), 488-89.
11. Ibid. 557.

already put into his *Physical and Medical Climate* (one reviewer thought their high moral tone ridiculous).[12] In the section on "Drink" he maintained that "it is a physiological fact that a man in good health does not require the use of wine or spirits, or any stimulating liquor." But he went on to recommend light wine, draught, rather than bottled, beer, and sherry and bitters for those in need of strengthening. Brandy he recommended only if administered by a doctor. A few years later, speaking in London, he said he advocated moderation in drinking in the tropics, rather than total abstinence.[13] But this was for Europeans. Speaking in 1879 to an African audience at a meeting organized in Cape Coast by a temperance society, the Advanced Guard Lodge of the Independent Order of Good Templars, he advocated total abstinence.[14] Here the racial approach to medicine, almost absent from his book, appeared empirically.

Horton had produced a practical comprehensive work. No doubt it was of value to contemporary practitioners. But its theoretical assumptions were soon outdated. Within a few decades the whole frame of reference for research into tropical medicine was to change utterly. His contributions—his correlation of soil, climate and disease, or his ozone theory—would appear irrelevant, if not laughable, to a generation that no longer believed malaria and cholera were caused by bad air. His work appears on the far side of a historical divide which seems almost to put him in company with the medical science of Arabic and European antiquity, rather than with that of the twentieth century. But if his book has ceased to be useful to doctors, it still remains of interest to historians of medicine.

LIFE AT CAPE COAST

Medical officers serving in West Africa were organized in 1870 into a separate African Medical Service. Pay scales were raised in

12. Review in the *British and Foreign Medico-Chirurgical Review,* reprinted in the *Independent,* Aug. 12, 1875. The second edition added what was called another appendix—in fact a new entry in the table of contents, tabulating the medical formulae scattered throughout the book.
13. *Journal of the Royal Society of Arts,* vol. xxx (1881–82), 783.
14. *West African Reporter,* May 21, 1879.

that year, giving Horton another two shillings a day. In 1873 he and Davies were promoted by seniority to the rank of surgeon, with a further pay rise, and in 1875 to surgeon-major with £438 a year.[15] Davies, who had been seconded to the colonial service in Sierra Leone, now returned to the army.

Horton had originally been commissioned in the army in September 1859, and presumably imagined that he would be promoted, after fifteen years, in September 1874. But the promotion was not officially gazetted until 1 April 1875. Meanwhile *Diseases of Tropical Climates* had been printed, with the date 1874 on the title page, and his rank already given as "Surgeon-Major." Publication was delayed into 1875, but the book must have come out before April, as the word "Major" was struck out in ink.

He now remarried. His first marriage had connected him with the prominent Freetown recaptives: his second brought him into the "old families." His second wife, Selina Beatrice Elliott, was the granddaughter of one of the original settlers from Nova Scotia, the Reverend Antony Elliott, pastor of the Huntingdonian Church, an English Methodist offshoot, founded by Selina, Countess of Huntingdon. Selina Elliott's father was resident magistrate of one of the rural districts. Her mother was the daughter of a European trader who had been a member of the Governor's Council with the style of "Honorable."

In the past the Nova Scotian families had despised recaptives and their children. In *West African Countries* Horton wrote with great bitterness of their pretentious arrogance—and of how they preferred their daughters to be Europeans' mistresses rather than recaptives' wives. But, he went on, "the liberated Africans proved to be capable of far greater powers of improvement than they were, and in turn looked down on them, but more in pity and compassion than in disdain."[16] Now, apparently, he was ready to overlook past slights—even the illegitimate European connexion—and choose himself a Nova Scotian wife.

At the beginning of the Ashanti War he had turned up in Freetown, and there were rumours that he had come to meet his

15. *Army List,* July, 1870; *Royal Warrant,* 1870; *Army Lists,* 1873, 1875.
16. Horton, *West African Countries,* 26-27.

fiancée, nearly seventeen years his junior, who was just home from school in England. But he had been ordered back to headquarters after three weeks, and it was over a year before he could be spared from his medical duties to return and marry.

About six weeks before the day fixed for the marriage the bride's grandmother died. Then her mother fell ill—and died actually on the proposed wedding day. The postponed festivities were overshadowed by mourning. They were married in St George's Cathedral, for though the Elliotts were the mainstay of the Huntingdonian Church, like most of the Freetown elite they liked a stylish cathedral marriage. The bridegroom was in his major's uniform, the bride in a dress of rich white corded silk, trimmed with French lace and orange blossom, and a gold tiara studded with diamonds; the six bridesmaids were in pink and white. After champagne and cake at the Elliott residence they went off on honeymoon, first to a nearby country villa, then to Teneriffe.[17]

On his return to Cape Coast he rented a large house, Hamilton House, to live in. There their daughter, Nannette Susan Adelina, was born in May 1876.[18] His life was now more settled. When the civil government moved to Accra in 1877, army headquarters remained at Cape Coast. Though he more than once visited Lagos, he could no longer, as a senior officer, be pushed around to remote outstations.

Inevitably he was drawn into the social and legal squabbles of the Cape Coast community. During 1874 he was engaged in a series of complicated, but ultimately unsuccessful, lawsuits against Samuel Davis, a wealthy Fanti trader, over an unpaid doctor's bill.[19] When Mrs. Davis brought a divorce suit against her husband, he tried to implicate Horton in the proceedings by producing a witness, a former servant of Horton's, who was alleged to have declared that Mrs. Davis had committed adultery with him. But the judge ruled out what was a purely hearsay allegation.[20]

17. *Independent,* June 24, 1875; *African Times,* July 1, 1875, Aug. 2, 1875.
18. *African Times,* July 1, 1876.
19. Ghana National Archives, S.C.T. 5/4/44, case dated June 2, 1874; S.C.T. 5/4/99, cases dated June 29, 1874, Aug. 28, 1874, Sept. 2, 1874, Sept. 22, 1874.
20. S.C.T. 5/4/99, pp. 142-44, 182.

He also interested himself in the affairs of his friend George Blankson (whom he had once proposed for King of Fanti). Blankson was a member of the Colony Legislative Council, with an old established trading business at Anomabu. He had close ties with Ashanti and often went there on diplomatic missions for the colonial government. When the Ashanti invasion of 1873 began he joined the Fanti camp with his followers, but was at once accused of having treacherously conspired against his own people. Roused into a passion of war hysteria, the Fanti would have killed him, had a passing British official not sent some police to save him. He was arrested and sent to Cape Coast, where he was detained in the castle. Eventually released, his case was not investigated until the war was over. Not until April 1874 was he given a chance to clear himself. No witnesses appeared against him, and after another two months the case was dismissed.[21]

Among his accusers was James Hutton Brew, another Anomabu man, who had been secretary to the Fanti Confederation. He practised as a lawyer in Cape Coast and founded a newspaper there, the *Gold Coast Times*. He was a patient of Horton's—who took him to court in 1874 to make him pay a four-year-old doctor's bill.[22] Blankson, once cleared, brought a civil action for £3500 against the kings and chiefs who had accused him and against their advisers, including Brew.

The case was heard by a magistrate who awarded Blankson £2000 damages. It was then appealed and the judgment was reversed, as it was held that he had not technically proved damage. In a further statement the court declared him exonerated of the charges originally brought against him, and ordered each party to pay its own costs.

Horton was closely concerned with the case. Brew, who gave it great publicity in the *Gold Coast Times*, alleged that he had acted as Blankson's "(il)legal" adviser, directing the case behind the scenes. This was not unexpected. None of the lawyers prac-

21. P.R.O., C.O. 96/112, Strachan, 136, Dec. 3, 1874, and pamphlet enclosed.
22. Ghana National Archives, S.C.T. 5/4/44, case dated May 23, 1874. The case is mentioned in Margaret Priestley, *West African Trade and Coast Society* (London, 1969), 163.

tising in the courts (not even Brew) had any formal legal training, and Horton might be supposed as competent as they were to
draft a legal document. But what Brew printed in his paper as a
sample of Horton's drafting contained not only legal but gram-
matical errors: "if it is to be accepted as a specimen of the
learned doctor's grammar then we are afraid that his works must
occasion the printers no small amount of trouble." He went on to
suggest that not only had Horton lost the case for Blankson, but
that he had privately boasted beforehand that they were sure to
win, as he was "hand-in-glove" with the magistrate, a British
army officer.[23]

Brew belonged to one of the Anglo-Fanti "old families," as
proud of his royal birth as of his English education. He was
therefore inclined to think Horton an upstart. Horton had said
of himself in the preface to his *Letters on the Political Condition of the Gold Coast* that he was "descended from the royal
blood of Isuama Eboe," a claim that might have impressed readers in England, and might even have been true—but anyone in
West Africa knew that his parents had been slaves. Brew took
the chance of publicly deflating the social pretensions of "His
Royal Highness of Iswerma Eboe," and his assertive knowall
ways, in the *Gold Coast Times*.

All Africans ought to be proud of him, and we have no doubt they
are; but his pompous, assuming airs and bearing, and his constant
intermeddling with affairs in which he is in no way concerned, ill-
become *him* of all men. A man who rises from nothing deserves great
credit; but then for him to attempt to look down on his betters is simply
to make himself ridiculous; and the learned doctor does at times raise
one's risible faculties by his bearing. Although force of intellect and
wealth can break down all social distinctions, yet, nevertheless, such is
human nature that if a man of the lowest grade of society were to be
picked up, educated on charity, and raised himself subsequently to
some distinction, if he were to be pompous and to give himself airs, he
would be reminded of the position from which he had been dragged, although such would not be in accordance with good taste. We hope,
therefore, that Dr AFRICANUS HORTON will bear the consequences of
his own acts with all due meekness, and that he will in future refrain
from meddling in affairs not his own.[24]

23. For this case see *Gold Coast Times*, Sept. 30, 1874, Mar. 31, 1875, May 22,
1875, June 9, 1875, and *Independent*, Apr. 22, 1875, May 27, 1875.
24. *Gold Coast Times*, May 22, 1875.

Horton was spared the full impact of this public rebuke, for it appeared in the *Gold Coast Times of* 22 May 1875, when he was away in Freetown for his marriage.

Brew's animosity against him seems to have lingered. A couple of years later the choir of Christ Church, Cape Coast, was giving a Christmas Eve concert. Horton was chairman. Some drunken Europeans came in, made a disturbance, and ridiculed him. Brew, who would normally have been quick to reprobate such conduct, merely reported it in his paper as a harmless piece of high spirits, "a lark (to use a vulgarism)."[25]

Life in this small garrison town, with its petty feuds and snobberies, restricted social contacts, and lack of intellectual stimulus, offered little to a man of Horton's energy and imagination. Increasingly, he became preoccupied with projects that stretched far beyond its narrow limits.

HORTON AS ENTREPRENEUR

Horton's interest in geology was not limited to correlating the incidence of morbidity and soil formation. He perceived that West Africa was rich in unexploited or underexploited mineral resources which could be developed for the enrichment of its people. In Sierra Leone iron ore had been worked on a small scale for many centuries. His own soil analysis looked forward to large-scale production—but it was not until the 1930's that mining was intensively developed there.

At Keta in 1860 he had studied the shellfish in the lagoon. "I was forcibly struck," he wrote later "with their resemblance and identity with those on the coast of the Brazils." He found many botanical similarities too, and near identity of geological structure.

These facts led me to the belief that when the resources of the country are much more developed *diamonds* will be found, not only in the Eastern District, but also in the rivers and lagoons of Awoonah and Dahomey. I made fruitless searches myself whilst stationed at Quittah and Addah, but it is my firm belief that in years to come, all things

25. *Gold Coast Times,* Dec. 27, 1877.

being equal, and development progressive, the diamond will ultimately be one of the exportable articles.[26]

It was nearly forty years after his death that diamonds were
found, in a tributary of the Pra; by the mid-1930's over a million
carats were being exported annually. His prophecy that "there
are extensive *coal-fields* in the interior of the country and in the
kingdom of Dahomey" remains as yet unconfirmed.

Over a large area inland from the coast round Axim, between
the mouths of the Pra and the Ankobra rivers, alluvial gold had
been mined for export for many centuries. It was obtained from
near the surface by digging and washing. The kings who controlled the deposits guarded production as a state-regulated enterprise. Foreigners were not permitted to mine. In 1861 Thomas
Hughes, a West Indian living at Cape Coast, imported machinery
from Europe and began mining in Western Wassaw, hoping to
work the deeper strata. No sooner had his workmen reached a
rich vein than the king turned him out of the country and destroyed his machinery. Horton was enraged by what he could
only see as an obscurantist policy designed to frustrate economic
development.[27]

Europeans, too, dreamed of a gold rush to West Africa. From
the early 1860's Fitzgerald had extolled it in the *African Times*
as richer than California, then world famous for its gold. Burton
entitled a chapter of his *Wanderings,* "Gold in Africa." The jour-
nalists who accompanied Wolseley's expedition alerted a wider
public to this potential source of wealth. Fitzgerald's enthusiasm
revived. In a leading article, entitled "The Ashanti War—Gold,
Gold, Gold!," he dreamed in his euphoric style of a gold rush to
Ashanti which would "found a civilized empire, where now the
ruthless vampire of a horrible superstition is daily consuming the
life-blood of countless victims."[28] Fitzgerald, like most British
contemporaries, could deplore that the Ashanti practised human
sacrifice, without apparently reflecting that their own government had been ready to sacrifice their own human countrymen
to fight them.

26. Horton, *West African Countries,* 134-35.
27. Horton, *West African Countries,* 238-39.
28. *African Times,* Oct. 30, 1873.

During the Ashanti War Joseph Dawson, a Fanti who had been closely associated with the Fanti Confederation, was detained at Kumasi (where he had been sent on a mission by the colonial government), along with some German missionaries and a young French trader, Marie-Joseph Bonnat. When Bonnat returned to France after his release, Dawson wrote to him suggesting that he try and raise capital to mine gold on a large scale.[29] After some delay Bonnat and some French associates visited the Ankobra country with Dawson and obtained a twelve-mile concession from one of the rulers. On his return to Paris he formed the African Gold Coast Company Ltd., with an Anglo-French directorate, to send out heavy machinery to work the concession in depth.[30] Other prospective concessionaires followed.

The concession principle was nothing new in coastal West Africa. For centuries Europeans had been allowed trading privileges and land for forts in return for recognized payments. What was new in the mining concessions was the proposal to extract large quantities of gold by machinery, to which African rulers had hitherto objected. Presumably they were won over by the lure of cash payments and the promise of future royalties. Though the money involved was small, a few hundred pounds at most, it represented far more than they could make themselves using traditional methods. Also, some preferred dealing with a single concessionaire, rather than try and exact payments from the crowds of African surface operators who now flocked from other parts of the country, even from Sierra Leone.

The government, in London and on the coast, was uneasy at the prospect. Timid officials proved less adaptable than traditional rulers. Ready enough to increase colonial revenue by extending the familiar import-export trade, they feared the added responsibilities of a gold rush. The legal status of the Protectorate was still uncertain. They were afraid of a vast influx of European prospectors who would be out of control of the government and might well provoke wars and disturbances. Governor Freeling,

29. Jules Gros, *Voyages, Aventures et Captivité de J. Bonnat* (Paris, 1884), 264; R. F. Burton and V. L. Cameron, *To the Gold Coast for Gold* (London, 1883), vol. ii, p. 237.
30. P.R.O., C.O. 96/123, Freeling, 80, Apr. 27, 1878; C.O. 96/129, Wray, Mar. 11, 1879.

commenting on one of Fitzgerald's many blasts to the Colonial Office, enunciated the cautious conservative principles which were subsequently to guide British colonial policy in the era of "Indirect Rule"—that the Protectorate should go on being ruled in familiar ways, and that reforms should only be introduced "by as slight a disruption of long-cherished powers and customs as possible." Armed with this opinion, the Colonial Office could inform Fitzgerald that they were not prepared "to encourage or sanction any enterprise for the exploration of the supposed Gold Fields in the Gold Coast Colony."[31]

But though the government would not encourage prospectors and concession-seekers, it could not keep them out. Nor could it prevent them securing a legal status for their concessions by registering them at the Supreme Court Registry in Cape Coast. By 1880 at least four mining companies were actively operating. Others had been formed to buy and sell concessions on the London stock exchange. Fitzgerald was in the forefront, sponsoring and advertising companies. He renamed his paper *The African Times and Gold Coast Mining and Railway Chronicle*, and poured forth articles month after month prophesying great wealth for those who bought Gold Coast mining shares, and great benefit to Africa from the consequent diffusion of wealth and Christian civilization.

Horton, meanwhile, was putting his geological expertise to practical use. During April, May, and June of 1878 he went round the country inland from Axim persuading rulers to grant him mining concessions. In 1880 he or his agent, Frank Swanzy Essien, a young man from Dixcove, obtained more—at least twenty-six in all. He chose places where the ground had already been worked on the surface (one had the remains of ancient Portuguese or Dutch workings), or where his own geological knowledge predicted gold.

The leases were registered at Cape Coast, the forms of the leases varying. Most leased the land with exclusive rights to mine, build, cut timber, and construct railways for a period of 21 or of 50 years, with options to renew or cancel, for an annual

31. P.R.O., C.O. 96/114, Gregson, May 18, 1874, minutes; C.O. 96/121, Freeling, 143, May 29, 1877; C.O. 96/122, *African Times*, Apr. 9, 1877, minutes; Strachan, Sept. 27, 1877, minutes.

rent, varying from £80 to £200 a year, part paid at once in cash, the rest from when the mining operations began. Some added an annual 3 per cent royalty on profits. Some permitted African surface mining to continue.[32] Altogether Horton must have paid out about £1000 in cash payments for these leases.

Early in 1880 the Gold Coast Mining Company was formed in London, with Fitzgerald as secretary, to exploit Horton's most promising concession, Abontiakoon, near Tarkwa, where most of the mining companies congregated. The company purchased the concession from him and Fitzgerald (who may have helped him to finance the initial outlay of paying for the leases), though they preserved an interest as shareholders. Employees were sent out in May to start work, and the following year the *African Times* was reporting the discovery of extremely rich ore.[33]

These gold deposits could not be efficiently worked without mechanized transport. Fitzgerald regularly demanded in the *African Times* that railways be constructed (in articles that might be headed "The Spread of Christian Civilization in West Africa"). In 1879, in association with an English engineer who had some West African experience, he formed at least two companies to build railways to link the mining areas with the sea coast. The Colonial Office, always suspicious of concession-mongering, refused help.[34] Horton, at Fitzgerald's request, undertook the laborious task of personally making a rough survey of the country from Tarkwa to the coast. Eventually he drew up a plan of what he felt was the best route for a railway line—supporting his judgment by acquiring for himself some of the land it would have to cross.[35]

Suddenly, within a couple of years, he had been transformed from a routine-centred army doctor and magistrate into a far-sighted company promotor and entrepreneur, ready, as his retirement from the army approached, to embark on a new career of a completely different kind.

32. P.R.O., C.O. 879/46, pp. 5-10; see also Horton's will.
33. *African Times,* Feb. 2, 1880, Aug. 2, 1880, Aug. 1, 1881; P.R.O., C.O. 96/130, Ussher, 40, Feb. 4, 1880.
34. P.R.O., C.O. 96/128, Fitzgerald (n.d.), minutes; C.O. 879/38, pp. 27-31.
35. *African Times,* Jan. 2, 1882, Feb. 1, 1882; see also Horton's will, clause 92.

RETIREMENT FROM THE ARMY

He was transferred in July 1879 to army headquarters in Freetown, and arrived home with his wife and family to settle there after a long absence. But his stay was brief. After only a few weeks, he received sudden orders from London to return at once to Cape Coast as head of the Army Medical Department in the Gold Coast Colony. He and Davies had now served twenty years in the army and ranked as lieutenant-colonels (though still bearing the same title "Surgeon-Major"). By the following year they were the two senior officers in the African Medical Service. If they chose they could serve another five years.[36]

But Horton seems to have preferred the attractions of the business career that was awaiting him even to remaining as head of the Medical Department. Family ties, too, drew him back to Freetown, for his wife had remained there in 1879. On 4 December 1880 he retired from the army on half-pay. Davies followed his example and retired in September 1881. Under revised pension scales that came into force that year they were entitled to £365 a year.[37]

Shortly before he left Ghana to return finally to Sierra Leone Horton received an unexpected recognition of his services, not from the British government, which he had so loyally served, but from the Ashanti, against whom he had been twice opposed in war. Over the years he had become acquainted with Osoo Ansah, a member of the Ashanti royal family, educated in England, who lived in Cape Coast and often acted as an intermediary between the Asantahene and the British government. On 18 June 1879 he wrote to Horton—

Sir—His Majesty the King of Ashantee has heard with much pleasure the great interest you have always taken in the material advancement of his people and country, and the prompt assistance you rendered to the great Chief of Manipom, when written to about the chief's

36. *West African Reporter,* July 23, 1879, Aug. 27, 1879; *Watchman,* Aug. 30, 1879.
37. W. Johnston, *Roll of Army Medical Service* (London, 1917), nos. 5903, 5904; *Royal Warrant,* dated Mar. 11, 1882 (effective from July 1, 1881), section 982.

sufferings who had been laid up for such a long time.

His Majesty the King has also been informed of your endeavors extended over several years towards the general improvement of your countrymen throughout the whole coast, and expresses the hope that you may yet continue to be of great service to them.

His Majesty is informed that you are likely to leave the Gold Coast shortly, and not to return to it. He has therefore commissioned me to offer for your acceptance the *Title and Dignity of a Prince,* and trust that wherever you may be stationed you will continue to manifest great interest in Ashantee affairs.

I can assure you that I congratulate you at this offer from the King, and having known you for several years, and personally acquainted with your views, and endeavours for Ashantee, I consider it a fitting offer to you from my King, King Mensah of Ashantee.[38]

Though he did not normally use his Ashanti title, he was sometimes referred to in the newspapers as "Prince Horton."

HORTON'S WILL

He found another outlet for his financial ambitions on the London stock market. It was a period when the market was flooded with dubious but attractive-looking shares, heavily depreciated in value and priced well below par, to be bought by speculators hoping for a rise. Through the army agent in London from whom he received his pay (Sir Charles McGrigor & Co.) he acquired securities with face value of over £25,000—Hungarian, Peruvian, Egyptian, and Turkish government bonds, shares in a Chilean copper mine, in the Verna Railway, and in the Roumanian and Imperial Ottoman Banks.[39] He looked forward to these depreciated stocks increasing in value and providing a good investment for the future.

Before leaving Cape Coast he made a long will, disposing of what appeared to be a very substantial estate—securities in London nominally valued at £25,000, his mining and railway interests, and house property in Freetown.[40] He provided hand-

38. *West African Reporter,* Sept. 8, 1883.
39. They are enumerated in his will. "Verna" may be a miswriting of Varna, Bulgaria.
40. Copies of his will in Somerset House, London, Wills, vol. 627, no. 75 (1885), and in Registrar-General's Office, Freetown, Wills, vol. 3, pp. 111-29 (1883).

somely for his wife and two daughters. Each was to have a Free-town house and a large capital sum invested in trust, with the stipulation that should either daughter have a legitimate son who would hyphenate the name "Horton" with his father's name, he should inherit all his mother's estate. He gave legacies (mostly £50 to £100) to forty-three named individuals—friends in Cape Coast (J. H. Brew was included, as well as George Blankson), Lagos, and Freetown. His wife's relatives, the El-liotts, were not forgotten, nor his former mother-in-law, Mrs. Pratt, nor his putative half-sister, nor a Mrs. Mary Ann Cole of Gloucester and her son. He left £100 to Ferdinand Fitzgerald's daughter, and the copyright of his books to his old mathematics teacher, the Reverend George Nicol, who had grown up at Gloucester, and was now Colonial Chaplain in the Gambia.

He included bequests to the educational and religious estab-lishments he had been connected with—Fourah Bay College and the Sierra Leone Grammar School, also the recently founded Wesleyan Boys' High School in Freetown. There were bequests to the Sierra Leone Church and its missionary society, to the Church Missionary Society and the Wesleyan Missionary Society. Even the Huntingdonian Church was remembered.

For years he had dreamed of seeing established in Freetown an institution offering scientific and technological education. In his will he endowed it—Horton's Collegiate High School.

> It is my desire that the aim of this school should be the introduction of high scientific classes of study (mineralogy, geology, botany and allied sciences) and that every effort should be made to advance the standard of education in the school and to cause the said school to be affiliated to an English University.

If so affiliated, it would be renamed "Horton's College." But though it was to provide a scientific education, the instruction would be "based on the religious principles of the Church of England," and the trustees were to be the Bishop of Sierra Leone and four churchmen (two lay, two clerical). It was to be housed in his own Horton Hall, in central Freetown, as he thought out-of-town boarding establishments like Fourah Bay College unsuit-able for university education.

He had long been concerned to bring his Ibo countrymen

"into the employments of civilized Christian life." Several times he had tried unsuccessfully to bring boys from the Niger country to Freetown or Lagos for education. But, as a Lagos newspaper put it,

> . . . the natives on the Niger would not allow their children to be trained in distant lands for fear of death, and should any such youth fall sick and die, whoever took them away from their native land would be held responsible.[41]

He had to be content with giving financial help to a Sierra Leone Ibo, the scholar and poet Christian Cole, who was studying law in London. But in his will he made a further attempt for the future, directing that two students from the Niger Mission, one an Ibo, and two from the Sierra Leone Colony, one of Ibo descent, should always be educated free of charge at Horton's Collegiate High School.

His will set a practical example of what he preached—that economic resources should be developed as a means to extend education. The wealth he hoped to gain from the mineral resources of West Africa was to be ploughed back for the good of its people. It also illustrated his own personality. His precise detailed concern to make an equitable distribution of his property must have cost him many hours of careful reflexion, as he weighed the claims of his many friends and of the various institutions to which he felt loyalty and affection. Nor was he ashamed to attach his own name to the college he hoped to found. Above all, he displayed confidence in the future—in the great wealth that would accrue to his estate from his investments, and in the existence of a society in West Africa where young men would be able to rise as he had done, by their talents.

41. *The Eagle and Lagos Critic,* Nov. 24, 1883.

VII

THE LAST YEARS

RETURN TO FREETOWN

THE SIERRA LEONE Horton returned to in 1881 was still disappointingly like the colony he had described in the 1860's. Far from being "within a short time . . . left to govern themselves," its people were still governed from London. The only constitutional change, the splitting of the West African Settlements in 1874, had brought them no nearer self-government. They were, as it happened, ruled by a medical man, Dr. Samuel Rowe, one of Horton's colleagues in the Army Medical Service—but he was a white governor, appointed from London, not a black constitutional king elected by themselves.

Nor had the hinterland been annexed to create the large viable state Horton demanded. All that the British government would allow was the extension of the Colony's frontiers along the adjacent coastline to bring it under customs jurisdiction. Meanwhile the French were advancing inland to the north: a boundary agreement signed in 1882 was to condemn Sierra Leone to be a small enclave within a vast French empire.

A crippling blow to his dreams was the severe economic depression which spread from Europe in the early 1870's. Sierra Leone, tied to overseas markets and dependent for revenue on customs duties, was helplessly dependent on the European economy. By the mid-1870's it was bankrupt, only kept going by a loan from the British government. Expenditure was cut to a minimum. Even when prosperity returned at the end of the decade there was no immediate change, for the surplus revenue had to be spent repaying the loan.

A few of his proposals had been carried out. Freetown had a piped water supply. Its sanitation had been improved, but not as radically as he wanted. Trees had been planted in the streets, diffusing "ozone"—but the inhabitants thought they diffused snakes and bad smells and gradually cut them down. A few people had built themselves houses in the hills, but only the army authorities had made any large-scale move, building barracks and a sanitarium on "Mount Aureol," as he had once suggested.

A far-sighted project of the type he envisioned had been begun in 1871 while the Colony was still prosperous—the construction of a deep-water quay in Freetown harbour, financed by a government loan raised in London. But the plan was inadequate, and the work ill-supervised. For an outlay of £50,000 nothing was built but a useless sea-wall; in addition, a local businessman had to be heavily compensated for damage to property during construction. As well as paying off the revenue loan to the British government, the Colony was now saddled with interest payments on a Harbour Works Loan which had done nothing to improve the harbour. Horton's warnings against piling up public debt had been disregarded. Sierra Leone (like the governments of Liberia, Egypt, and Tunis at that period) was caught in one of the alluring traps of the era of advancing imperialism, public indebtedness to European shareholders.

In the late 1860's the Sierra Leone government began, as Horton wanted, to accept some responsibility for education, left until then almost entirely to missionary societies and churches. But with the depression of the 1870's public expenditure on education stopped. It only began again, still on a very modest scale, in 1882. Horton's dream of introducing compulsory education and training up a literate population was as far off as ever.

His plan for a West African university had been taken up enthusiastically in 1872 by Edward Blyden, who was then in Freetown editing a newspaper, *The Negro,* and James Johnson. He wrote a long letter to *The Negro* in support of a proposal that he had been urging for so long.[1] Their university, however, would have been on a different model from his—based ultimately on their differing concepts of race. Horton looked to Europe for guidance. Blyden and Johnson rejected it. Horton's university, like those of Europe and America, would have trained up practical men to develop their country. Theirs was to be a community of black scholars, gathered from Africa and America, who would create and impart a distinctively African culture, drawing inspiration from the African interior, not from Europe.[2]

But even they needed financial help from Europeans to carry out their plan. They enlisted the support of Governor Hennessy, who expressed immense enthusiasm—but could give them no more practical help than he had given the Fanti Confederation.

The C.M.S. was alarmed by this agitation, which seemed to threaten their own Fourah Bay College. After Blyden left Freetown they decided to turn it into a university institution. They were encouraged to do so by a leading Freetown businessman, William Grant.[3] Grant, like Horton, was the son of an Ibo recaptive, and like him was enterprising and energetic, with a mind of his own. "Independent Grant," as he was called, was a member of the Colony legislature and realized that it was impossible to finance a university from public funds, and that the only alternative was to use the existing college. In 1876 it was affiliated to Durham University in England, which agreed to supervise examinations and award degrees.

This university college was not the kind of university Horton had envisioned—a centre of scholarship and research, equipped to teach the natural sciences as well as the humanities. Though two of the first students were prepared for a medical education in Britain, scientific studies soon vanished from the curriculum. There was therefore still room in Freetown for the institution he was proposing to endow in his will.

Yet he had no need to despair if a locust decade had produced

1. Quoted in T. J. Thompson, *The Jubilee and Centenary Volume of Fourah Bay College* (Freetown, 1930), 54.
2. *The West African University* (Freetown, 1872) (copy in P.R.O., C.O. 267/ 317); see also Hollis R. Lynch, *Edward Wilmot Blyden* (London, 1967), 95-96; E. A. Ayandele, *Holy Johnson* (London, 1970), 72-73.
3. C.M.S., CAI/023, Grant, Oct. 1, 1874.

only a meagre harvest. Freetown was still the centre of a thriving articulate Creole community. William Grant and the other wealthy businessmen formed a solid black bourgeoisie who were leading on a modest scale the kind of lives lived by their white bourgeois contemporaries in Europe and America. Creoles filled the professions—the church, education, law—and produced the Freetown newspapers. Others had followed Horton into the medical profession. The most recent medical graduate, John Farrell Easmon, a relative of his second wife's, after a brilliant student career in London, was appointed a government doctor in the Gold Coast where he was to rise to be head of the medical service.[4] Like Horton, he carried on research, and isolated blackwater fever as a specific disease.[5]

Horton in 1881 could still have maintained, as he had in 1868, that "there is growing in Sierra Leone an enlightened population," and could still have looked forward as he had then to the ultimate emergence of a self-governing state.

BANKING AND MINING PROJECTS

He settled down with his family in Horton Hall, his imposing four-storied mansion which stood back from Gloucester Street in a garden full of oleanders. All around were similar houses, the homes of the substantial Freetown bourgeoisie. His colleague Davies settled near by in George Street in another large house. He too had married into high society: his wife, Mary Smith, was the daughter of the former Registrar of the Mixed Commission Court, and her brothers and brothers-in-law were mostly doctors and lawyers. He lived on quietly in Freetown, practising privately as a doctor, but taking little part in public life, a gentle, dignified, unobtrusive figure, until he died aged seventy-five in 1906.

4. For his career, see Lamin Abdou Mbye, "Senior African Civil Servants in British West Africa, 1808-95," unpublished Ph.D. thesis, University of Birmingham, 1969.
5. In my *A History of Sierra Leone,* I wrote (p. 423) that "his work on blackwater fever was the first original contribution made by an African doctor to European medical science." Plainly, I was unfair to Horton, whose work was also original, though it turned out less useful to medical research than Easmon's.

Horton's life in retirement was to be very different—continually occupied with one project or another, always active, busy, and self-assertive. The story is told that one day a white soldier in the Freetown garrison in some way overlooked the presence of the little doctor. He hurried home and put on his full dress lieutenant-colonel's uniform, then returned and made the soldier stand to attention, salute, and apologize.[6]

Writers on Sierra Leone regularly deplored that the Colony peninsula was not more intensively farmed: Horton had taken up the theme in *West African Countries and Peoples*. When he was in Freetown for his second marriage in 1875 he had applied to the government for a grant of 100 acres to cultivate when he retired.[7] But by 1881 this project was forgotten, or postponed, for something more ambitious and original.

Credit, even cash, was always in short supply in the West African export centres. The Freetown business community, tied to an import-export economy, had to raise and remit money through agents in England. The Freetown banks were small-scale money-lending establishments, usually run as a sideline to other business, advancing small loans at high rates of interest. During the produce-buying season, when cash was scarce, they might charge businessmen up to 30 per cent.

Several attempts had been made over the previous decade to found a bank to provide credit on better terms, but they came to nothing—if only because of the opposition of the European firms, who feared to lose their hold on the credit supply.[8] In *West African Countries* Horton had recommended that the government found a national bank. After fourteen years a government savings bank was belatedly opened, attached to the post office, but a purely deposit bank without credit facilities. He therefore determined to supply the deficiency himself, and on the basis of his own financial resources, to found a bank in Freetown with branches along the coast.

Fortuitously, the government had just made his project safer

6. I was told this story by Dr. Davidson Nicol, who had it from the late Mr. Justice R. W. B. Marke.

7. Sierra Leone Archives, C.S.O.R. 1179/1875.

8. *West African Reporter,* Mar. 10, 1883.

by demonetizing the Spanish and American dollars, sometimes forged and usually overvalued, which circulated in West Africa, thereby establishing a more reliable currency.[9] He proposed to run his establishment purely as a bank, not as an adjunct to other commercial speculations, to advance credit to business people and farmers, and encourage the economic development of the country—always his ultimate aim.

Soon after his arrival in Freetown from Cape Coast he fell ill. He recovered slowly. In March he was still unable to receive a deputation of townsmen from Gloucester who came to present an address of welcome. But by early July he was well enough to leave for England with his wife and youngest daughter to organize his banking, mining and railway interests.[10]

Fitzgerald was still printing enthusiastic mining reports in the *African Times*. The Gold Coast Mining Company which he and Horton had sponsored was by now operating in Abontiakoon. The first manager, who had had the initial task of clearing the bush, had been superseded, and a new, more energetic, successor sent out. Though their working capital was small they felt sure of a good return, and were encouraged to float at least two more companies—the Wassaw and Ahanta Gold Mines Syndicate and the Tacquah Gold Mines Company Ltd—to exploit Horton's other concessions.[11] They also formed a railway syndicate, subsequently registered as the Wassaw Light Railway Company Ltd, to construct a railway to service the existing mines, and ultimately extend into the far interior and open up "the region of the grand auriferous reefs in the Kong Mountains."[12]

Horton's Ibo countryman William Grant was also in London organizing ambitious development projects. A largely self-educated businessman three or four years older than Horton, he shared his desire to develop unused West African resources. Having made money out of import-export trading, he turned

9. P.R.O., C.O. 879/18, Correspondence relating to the Currency of the West African Colonies and St Helena, 1883.

10. *West African Reporter,* Mar. 26, 1881, July 9, 1881. Before leaving he may have had one of his rare meetings with Dr. Blyden, who visited Freetown in May 1881 (*Watchman,* May 30, 1881).

11. P.R.O., C.O. 879/46, pp. 2-11.

12. *African Times,* Jan. 2, 1882; *West African Reporter,* July 7, 1883.

to plantation farming, and came to London to buy sugar processing machinery, to start up a Sierra Leone sugar industry. Among his other projects was buying machinery to manufacture ice and soda water, necessary commodities in a tropical city, which were still not manufactured in Freetown.[13]

But his various schemes took longer to arrange than he had intended. His stay dragged on into winter, and he had to be out in all weathers visiting his business contacts. Despite Horton's medical attentions he became seriously ill, and he died in a London hotel in January 1882. Horton, writing his obituary in the *African Times,* recalled how his old mentor Henry Venn had originally introduced Grant to Fitzgerald, twenty years before, with the words—"Here is my *beau ideal* of an African"[14]— for a man like "Independent Grant," with his tall distinguished appearance, his success in business, his high principles and hard work, justified to Venn his faith in African capabilities.

In London Horton just missed a public confrontation with his old antagonist Captain Richard Burton. From the period of his stay in West Africa Burton had dreamed of gold, and was determined to take part in any European gold rush there. Early in 1882 he visited the Ankobra country, accompanied by another of the European "explorers" of Africa, Captain V. L. Cameron. They were very careful to assert their status as gentlemen-travellers—but their excursion was in fact paid for by a Liverpool mine owner. Burton fell ill after a few weeks and went home, but Cameron travelled round the mines taking careful note of all he saw.

The Royal Society of Arts, a London society founded to spread technological information, booked Burton to speak on "The Gold Fields of West Africa." At the last moment he sent word that he was too ill to come, and Cameron had to speak instead. Lord Alfred Churchill, formerly of the African Aid Society, was in the chair. Horton was in the audience.

Cameron gave a brief unprepared talk, stressing the great potential wealth of the country. Horton then rose and, speaking at length, confirmed what Cameron had said about the wealth

13. *West African Reporter,* Aug. 6, 1881, Feb. 25, 1882.
14. *African Times,* Feb. 1, 1882.

of this "new California." He described in some detail the vicissitudes of the mining companies, pointing out that they were still in the pioneer stage and could not be expected to pay large dividends immediately. Of the Gold Coast Mining Company, with which he was closely concerned, he said "that it stood almost above the others, because the amount of gold in the quartz reef ranged nearly £4 to the ton."

One of the mine operators' most difficult problems was securing a regular non-seasonal labour supply, in a country where labour was seasonally tied to subsistence farming. Cameron proposed that Chinese coolies be introduced, using the racial argument that they were a "persevering race," which by implication Africans were not. This argument omitted to mention that imported labourers—whether African slaves on American plantations, or Chinese coolies down African mines—are forced to be "persevering." Horton, however, assured the audience that adequate mine labour could be recruited in the Kru country of Liberia, where for at least a hundred years the men had been accustomed to leave home and work for wages along the coast. For the benefit of European mine employees, he concluded with a few words on a subject he had long studied—the effect of climate on health—pointing out that if they lived regular abstemious lives, and looked after themselves, they should have little to fear.

Desultory conversation followed. A retired general from the Army Medical Department, ignoring what Horton had just said, rambled on about the deadly climate. A Scottish trader who had lived thirty-one years in West Africa retorted that it was not deadly to those who were not afraid of hard work. A gentleman reminisced about his brother, who had once lived 170 miles north of Timbuktu. Another inquired how far down the gold seams were—but a practical question of this kind Cameron was not prepared to answer.[15]

Next week Burton had recovered and gave his talk—but Horton seems not to have been in the audience. Neither speaker defamed educated Africans: Cameron may have been restrained

15. *Journal of the Royal Society of Arts,* xxx (1881-82), 777-85.

by Horton's presence. But they made up for it in a book they published jointly later in the year, *To the Gold Coast for Gold*. Burton's garrulous, disorganized contribution included two long chapters vilifying Sierra Leone, much of it repeated verbatim from his *Wanderings*. Cameron considered it intolerable that "Anglo-Niggers" should presume to work the gold deposits for themselves. Both sneered at Horton (though Cameron had not dared to insult him to his face), implying that he and Fitzgerald were merely fraudulent company promoters, and pointing out (quite correctly) that his proposed railway would run across land he had acquired for himself.[16]

SICKNESS AND DEATH

Horton and his wife spent fourteen months in England, living at 40 St Luke's Road, Westbourne Park, then a fashionable part of West London.[17] His main objective, apart from getting medical treatment, was organizing the Commercial Bank of West Africa. As well as holding deposits on interest and supplying credit, the bank was to carry on the agency business which sustained Freetown commerce, collecting and transmitting bills of exchange drawn on firms in Europe, and transmitting money to and from Europe. He needed a reliable agent in London, and found one in the army agent through whom he received his pay and bought shares, the firm of Sir Charles McGrigor, Baronet, and Co., whose founder had inherited a title from his father, Sir James McGrigor, formerly Director-General of the Army Medical Department, which no doubt encouraged Horton and other army doctors to deal with him. In days when a baronetcy commanded high social esteem, this was a most respectable-sounding firm, particularly as it had a most respectable-sounding address, off St James's Square. He also retained a London solicitor, as well as the outstanding legal practitioner in Freetown, Samuel Lewis.[18]

16. R. F. Burton and V. L. Cameron, *To the Gold Coast for Gold* (London, 1883), vol. ii, pp. 115, 261, 271, 274, 291-93.
17. Registrar-General's Office, Freetown, Conveyances, vol. 32, p. 272.
18. Advertisements in *Watchman,* Jan. 10, 1883, *Freetown Express,* Apr. 6, 1883; for Lewis, see J. D. Hargreaves, *A Life of Sir Samuel Lewis*, London, 1958.

Such contacts gave his bank a backing of implicit reliability and distinction which put it into a completely different category from the existing Freetown loan banks and from the various dubious-looking ventures that had surfaced and vanished in the past.

On his return to Freetown in September 1882 he could at once prepare to open the bank. It started business on 15 January 1883 at Shaftesbury House, on the corner of Oxford and Rawdon Streets.[19] He may have intended to build his own premises eventually on a large vacant waterfront property adjoining the East Battery which he bought while he was in London.[20]

He carried on the business himself, engaging his employees locally and supervising them personally. In this way he avoided the expense and risk of importing European employees with banking experience who might easily prove unreliable. Knowing the Freetown community, he could evaluate the credit-worthiness of his customers himself, and smell out the fraudulent. But he was ready to advance credit, in one case over £1000, to those he believed were reliable, using mortgages on Freetown house property as a security for loans. His heaviest expense was importing supplies of coin in bulk from England. To offset it, he charged an interest rate of sixpence in the pound per month, a high rate, but still less than the loan banks charged.[21]

He returned also as a social figure. He and his wife, who brought back an English lady's maid, made Horton Hall a centre of Freetown society, setting a standard of Europeanized elegance for the Freetown elite to envy and emulate. Selina Horton had a beautiful singing voice ("marred," as one critic put it, "by a slight affectation"). She and her sister, Esther Elliott, regularly took part in charity concerts, singing popular ballads, sometimes accompanied on the piano by her step-daughter May. The Hortons were present at fashionable weddings and funerals. When an Elliott cousin married they provided a lavish reception. The

19. *Freetown Express*, Apr. 6, 1883.
20. Registrar-General's Office, Freetown, Conveyances, vol. 32, p. 272, conveyance dated July 31, 1882.
21. Ibid. Conveyances, vol. 38, pp. 51-66; *African Times*, Mar. 1, 1883; *Watchman*, Oct. 20, 1883.

two Horton step-sisters, May and Nannette, were bridesmaids "dressed in pink bedecked with choice flowers, each carrying a basket of flowers (themselves prettier flowers)"—and then, when the European-style celebrations were over, and the five-tiered wedding cake was eaten, *gumbe* dancers turned up to celebrate in African style.[22]

Their own entertainments, too, became more relaxed in tone as time passed. At their first "At Home," with the Governor of the Colony and his lady present, the guests arrived at half past four and conversed politely until six when they withdrew with bows and handshakes. Six months later there was music and dancing, "and the lively party kept up until half past three in the morning."[23]

Inevitably he was in constant demand to preside at school and church functions. He sat on the platform at the Wesleyan Female Institution Entertainment, where his daughter May played the piano, and the girls debated a theme that will have interested him, "Whether High Class Education for Women was of any advantage in Africa." At the Grammar School annual dinner he reminded his audience that "it should be our duty to advance the cause of Africa . . . by working hard, setting forth good examples, acting on moral principles and publishing works (cheers)"[24]

Always loyal to the church in which he had nearly become a pastor, he was elected a lay member of the supervisory Church Committee, and took charge of the church finances, going round personally to collect money for an endowment fund. Busy and active as ever, his days were filled with engagements.

It was believed in Freetown that educated Creoles tended to die young or in their prime. In the New Year's issue for 1883 the *West African Reporter*, the leading Freetown newspaper, rehearsed a long list of recent deaths. They included the proprietor of the paper, William Grant, just predeceased by his son and followed soon after by his widow, the Reverend James Quaker, the Principal of the Grammar School, and Horton's

22. *West African Reporter*, Oct. 21, 1882.
23. *Watchman*, Jan. 10, 1883; *West African Reporter*, June 9, 1883.
24. *West African Reporter*, Dec. 16, 1882, May 5, 1883.

Gloucester contemporary Isaac Fitzjohn, the Postmaster. Dr. Davies's wife died soon after. There were no statistics to evaluate whether the death rate was high or low as compared with other parts of the world, for the systematic registration of births and deaths which Horton had advocated in 1868 was still neglected. Probably, with access to medical care, they lived longer than their Temne and Mende neighbours inland—though at a period when tropical medicine was still in its pioneer stage, they may have died younger than their middle-class contemporaries in Europe.

But deaths show up conspicuously in any small elite. As death struck down one prominent middle-aged Creole after another in the succeeding decades, the community came to feel that it was haunted by a fatal inborn crippling weakness that destroyed its sons before they had reached their full promise.

Horton had received the best medical treatment available during his long stay in London. Though his recovery was slow, he returned apparently in good health to his new exertions in Freetown. Up to the beginning of the second week in October he was regularly attending to his business at the bank every day. Then he was prostrated by severe erysipelas, a skin infection which can spread into the bloodstream and cause death.

By the end of the week he knew he was going to die. He gave orders to seal up his bank premises, and called in the acting Colonial Chaplain of the nearby Cathedral, the Reverend Philip Doughlin, a West Indian missionary of African descent, to give him the sacrament. His old friend Davies did what he could, but in vain. Horton knew he could not live, and, as a Freetown newspaper put it, he "faced death unflinchingly as becomes a christian soldier."[25] On Monday, 15 October 1883, at 8:30 in the evening, he died.

He was buried next day with the full ceremony of public pomp and grief. From the Cathedral, where the coffin lay in state, surrounded by a congregation of army officers, senior officials, and prominent townspeople, the funeral procession moved out, escorted by the police, and swelled as it went by a vast crowd. As

25. *Watchman*, Oct. 20, 1883.

they wound slowly up the grassy streets on their long way to the Circular Road Burial Ground, the bells of each church rang out as they passed the door—College Chapel, Zion, Ibo Baptist, Ebenezer, Lawson Church, Tabernacle—one after the other bidding farewell to their famous countryman.

In death as in life Africa and Europe blended. At the cemetery the screams and lamentations of the women, worked up to hysteria, even to fainting, as they mourned uninhibitedly, accompanied the slow restrained words of the burial service of the Church of England. His body was placed in the family tomb of his late father-in-law and Ibo compatriot, W. H. Pratt, beside his first wife, among his own people from a distant homeland beyond the Niger.[26]

THE DREAMS FADE

Horton's name was not inscribed on the Pratt family vault, but a tablet to his memory outlining his career (with his age given incorrectly) was put up in St. George's Cathedral. His more spectacular monument was his will. The Freetown public were amazed to hear of the lavish endowments and benefactions it detailed. Nothing like it had ever been seen in West Africa.

He had appointed five executors. Two were in England—his agent Sir Charles McGrigor (who renounced his executorship[27]), and a member of a London law firm which was concerned with his mining interests. Three were in Sierra Leone—William Grant, Charles Wilson Macaulay, and Moses Potts. Grant was already dead. Macaulay was an import-export trader, of the firm Macaulay Brothers in Water Street, a leading Freetown figure whose late father had been recognized by the Yoruba descendants as their king. Potts, a senior official in the Colonial Treasury, was a relative by marriage. His sister, Mrs. W. H. Pratt, had been the mother of Horton's first wife, Fannie. His own first wife had been an Elliott, Selina Horton's sister, but after her death he had married another Ibo descendant, Eleanor Fitzjohn.

26. *Freetown Express,* Oct. 19, 1883; *West African Reporter,* Oct. 20, 1883.
27. Registrar-General's Office, Freetown, Conveyances, vol. 37, p. 106.

Horton's Ibo relatives had got his body: now they disputed the disposition of his property. Potts brought a Chancery action against Mrs. Horton. Leading Freetown lawyers were engaged—for Potts, T. J. Thompson and A. S. Hebron, for Mrs. Horton, the Shorunkeh–Sawyerr brothers. Time mattered little in these Chancery lawsuits, some of which had been before the Sierra Leone courts for decades. Potts died in 1902 (Macaulay had already died in 1892), but his widow carried on the case unrelentingly.[28]

Part of Horton's estate was in England—the investments he had made on the London stock exchange, and in his own mining and railway companies. His English estate was valued at £3515.5.6.[29] This was a trifling sum in comparison with the £25,000 the stock exchange investments alone were purported to be worth, but it did not necessarily represent a loss, as he must originally have bought them up cheap. His executors and legatees could still hope, as he had done, that they and his mining and railway interests would eventually appreciate in value.

A few months before his death his Abontiakoon mine, worked by the Gold Coast Mining Company, was reported to be working successfully "on a moderate scale" after several changes of management. But the directors in London had little control over operations. They were persuaded to sink capital in another concession hawked to them by a returned mine manager. Then the company secretary disappeared with £200. Horton's Wassaw and Ahanta Gold Mining Syndicate became involved in litigation at Cape Coast. The grantors of one of the concessions maintained that they had not understood the terms; eventually judgment was given against the Syndicate.[30] By then Horton had died. Fitzgerald, whose enthusiasm had kept their projects before the public, died a few months after him.[31]

28. Apart from references in the Cause Book for 1904-12 I was not able to find any record of this case among the Supreme Court records in Freetown. I am grateful to Mr Reginald Clark, the Law Librarian, and to his clerk, Mr. Kenny, for helping me in my search.
29. Somerset House, London, Wills and Administrations, 1885, p. 627.
30. *West African Reporter*, June 16, 1883; Ghana National Archives, S.C.T. 5/4/98, pp. 3133-3136.
31. *African Times*, Mar. 1, 1884.

All the Gold Coast mining companies were in any case running into trouble, hampered by lack of a steady labour supply and of transport. Horton's Wassaw Light Railway Company sent out an engineer to make a systematic survey for a railway line. He advised against the route Horton had chosen, and invested in, and suggested an alternative route. But nothing came of this proposal or of other private railway projects.[32] Finally, in 1898, the government accepted responsibility, and built a line from Sekondi to Tarkwa—away from Horton's land.

Until a railway was built the mining companies could do little. By the end of the 1880's only one of them, Horton's Wassaw and Ahanta Gold Mining Syndicate, had ever paid a dividend out of profits—and that was from property sales, not from mining. The Abontiakoon mine was deserted, its machinery sold off for £120. All the companies he had been concerned with had failed.[33] Not until the Ashanti Goldfields Corporation was founded in 1897, and the railway extended to Obuasi in 1902, did gold mining again offer serious hopes of profit.

Nevertheless, for a short period Gold Coast mining shares appreciated immensely in value. During the Anglo-Afrikaner War in South Africa, speculators on the London stock exchange were unable to deal in South African mining shares. Instead they turned to what they called the "West African Jungle," and offered the public millions of pounds' worth of shares in West African mining and development companies. Over three hundred were floated during 1901, not to mine or to develop the country, but to buy and sell concessions and make a quick profit for the promoters. When the war ended and the Johannesburg stock exchange opened again, the West African boom ended abruptly.[34]

Had Horton's executors been able to realize the vastly inflated value of his concessions during the "West African Jungle" boom, his estate might have swelled to dimensions that even he could scarcely have dreamed of. But the lawsuit was still unsettled, the boom collapsed, and the concessions became so much waste paper.

32. P.R.O., C.O. 879/14, fols. 234, 282; C.O. 879/38.
33. Parliamentary Papers, 1889, vol. liv, pp. 175-87.
34. *African Times*, Aug. 3, 1901; *West African News* (London), 1901-1902.

Year after year the case of "Eleanor Elizabeth Potts, in lieu of Moses Abraham Potts *versus* Selina Beatrice Horton and others" dragged on. Thirty years after his death it was still before the courts. When it was finally settled there was not enough money to endow Horton's Collegiate High School. Instead the court directed that the residue be used to endow three scholarships at the Sierra Leone Technical School, founded by the Bishop of Sierra Leone to train artisans. In January 1915 an examination was held, and scholarships were awarded to learn "the theory and practice of the building trades and allied subjects."[35] This was a curriculum very different from the "high scientific classes of study (mineralogy, geology, botany and allied sciences)" that Horton had proposed—though it was one that most Europeans in Sierra Leone in 1915 would have felt was far more suited for Africans.

Once again his careful plans had come to nothing. His investments, his entrepreneurial schemes, his far-sighted educational proposals, had all faded away like his political blueprint for immediate self-government in British West Africa.

HORTON'S FAMILY

After Horton died his wife and two daughters went on living in Horton Hall. In 1888 the elder daughter, May, married François Turpin, a Senegalese, and went to live in Conakry. Her half-sister, Nannette, was sent to Europe to be educated, and stayed for five years in England and Germany.[36] Mrs. Horton turned Horton Hall into a private boarding house. An English lawyer and his wife who stayed there in 1898 thought poorly of it. "Breakfast beastly as usual," he commented in his diary, "very uncomfortable at Horton Hall." After a week they left. Mrs. Horton was indignant, "tearful—angry and abusive."[37]

Another of her English guests, W. H. Boucher, received a more

35. *Colony and Provincial Reporter,* Dec. 12, 1914, Jan. 30, 1915.
36. *Sierra Leone Weekly News,* June 23, 1888, June 19, 1897.
37. Private manuscript diary of G. A. Bonner, entries under Aug. 24, 1898, Aug. 26, 1898. I am grateful to Mr. and Mrs. C. F. C. Letts for allowing me to see this diary.

favourable welcome. He married Nannette, just back from Europe. Eventually they all left Freetown for England. Mrs. Horton died there, at Dover, in 1910. The Bouchers remained in England, hoping vainly to salvage something from the Horton fortune. After some unhappy experiences Nannette Boucher died in London in 1924, survived by her husband, four children (one of them named James Horton Boucher after his grandfather) and two grandchildren.[38] Her descendants did not return to live in Freetown. Horton Hall was sold to the government. Any dreams Horton may have had of founding a dynasty in Sierra Leone proved as illusory as his dreams of founding a technological university there.

38. *Sierra Leone Weekly News,* July 16, 1910, Sept. 20, 1924.

CONCLUSION

THE POLITICAL FUTURE

DURING THE LAST YEARS of Horton's life the European nations were beginning to close in on Africa. The French legislature voted credits for a trans-Saharan railway, British troops intervened in Egypt, Stanley was annexing the country south of the Congo for King Leopold, while on the north bank a Senegalese sergeant guarded the flag of France. Soon after Horton died the German government annexed Togo and Kamerun, and the Berlin Conference met to regularize procedures for the European partition of Africa. Within twenty years of his death it was complete. A new map of Africa had been drawn. As in the Anglo–Dutch treaty of 1867, the African populations were not consulted. The frontier lines were drawn in Europe. Instead of separating African states, as he had once envisioned, they formed prison bars delimiting European colonies and protectorates.

In these European possessions whites ruled and non-whites obeyed. All the European empires in Africa were empires of race, where there was little place for an educated African like Horton. Those with professional qualifications were squeezed out of government service and humiliated socially. His wife's relative Dr. J. F. Easmon was ruthlessly hounded out of his post as Chief Medical Officer, Gold Coast, by a vindictive governor and replaced by a European. Regulations were made in 1902 to constitute a unified West African Medical Service. Africans were specifically excluded from it, and relegated to a separate service, with lower salary scales, so that even the most senior African doctor could not give an order to the most junior white doctor.

A career like Horton's was now impossible. Burton and Hunt had triumphed. The "false theories of modern anthropologists," which he had denounced in 1868, were enthroned in the twentieth century as the guiding principles of empire.

Education, which he had seen as the key to African advancement, was neglected. Though the colonial governments and missionary societies supported a few schools, the vast majority of people in West Africa remained illiterate. The mass education he had dreamed of was utterly inappropriate in the colonial situation. Educated Africans were only wanted for subordinate clerkships. Nor did the colonial governments in West Africa put much energy into economic development. Administrative convenience was put first in these bureaucratically governed territories. Officials tended to follow the tradition of Governor Freeling, introducing innovation "by as slight a disruption of long-cherished powers and customs as possible." Their own bureaucratic "powers and customs" were entrenched as sacred instruments of policy.

The urgent sanitary reforms Horton had called for were also forgotten. "Hill Stations" and "cantonments" were built for the white officials, but little was done for the African population. Over seventy years after he had published his *Physical and Medical Climate*, another African research scientist, Sanya Onabamiro, published a book calling attention to the fearful lack of medical and sanitary services in West Africa, and demanding (as he had done) compulsory registration of births, deaths, and diseases as an essential prerequisite for the study of West African morbidity.[1]

Horton foresaw none of this. To the last he retained his faith in British benevolence. "I feel deeply," he said in 1881, "the gratitude I owe to the most civilized and generous Government in the world"[2]—a government that was to repudiate after his death everything he loved and strove for. For another sixty years arrogant, complacent, insensitive white governments were to

1. Sanya Dojo Onabamiro, *Why Our Children Die,* London, 1949.
2. *West African Reporter,* Mar. 26, 1881.

deny, or to notice only with grudging condescension, the aspirations he had voiced.

Yet in the long run his faith was justified. With the Second World War, British governments began to resume the tradition of the Parliamentary resolutions of 1865. Belatedly British policymakers adopted Horton's belief that "under the fostering care of the mother Government the people can, within a short time, be left to govern themselves."

During the 1940's and 1950's talented Africans were once again admitted to government service in British West Africa and promoted increasingly to the highest ranks. Money was spent, as he had demanded, on economic development, including education which was now seen, as he had seen it, as part of development. Universities were founded of the type he had advocated, with medical and technological departments, teaching to a high standard and stimulating research.

In 1957, with the creation of the independent state of Ghana, "Self-government of the Gold Coast" (a chapter heading in *West African Countries and Peoples*) was achieved. In 1960 the president of a republic was installed at Accra, as he had proposed nearly a century earlier—and a president who ruled in the authoritarian manner he was inclined to approve of. As the other British West African territories followed Ghana peacefully into independence, the future he had originally prophesied for his own lifetime was realized eighty years after his death.

HORTON IN HISTORY

When Horton died the Freetown and Lagos newspapers were full of lamenting obituaries (though Brew printed only a perfunctory notice in the *Gold Coast Times*). In Lagos D. B. Vincent, better known by the name he subsequently took, Mojola Agbebi, published a poem in his memory, predicting undying fame—

> Thy name shall be the people's song,
> Thy worth must claim the Negro's tongue,
> Thy works shall lead thy race along . . .[3]

3. *The Eagle and Lagos Critic*, Nov. 24, 1883.

In Freetown the veteran editor M. H. Davies proposed to write his biography, but gave up when he found how much space it would take up in his paper.[4] From time to time his name was recalled in the Sierra Leone press: as the colonial age darkened he was remembered as one of the "giants" of the golden age of the nineteenth century. His photograph was included, with a biographical sketch and extracts from his will, in a Fourah Bay College centenary volume published in 1930. But no serious study of his life appeared.

During the colonial era his memory was inevitably pushed into oblivion. Europeans, firm in the faith that Africans were incapable of any original accomplishment, would scarcely have believed it possible that an African could have written books and done independent research and risen to the rank of lieu-tenant-colonel in the British army. Those who mentioned him did not trouble to find out much about him. W. W. Claridge, who used his *Letters on the Political Condition of the Gold Coast* as a source for his *History of the Gold Coast and Ashanti,* a two-volume work published in 1915, referred to him briefly as "A native of the Gold Coast." His name did not appear in either of W. E. F. Ward's successive histories of Ghana, though Sir John Gray in his *History of the Gambia,* published in 1940, quoted his account of self-government on MacCarthy's Island.

Even politically conscious Ghanaians forgot him. In 1893, it is true, during the public outcry over the dismissal of Dr. J. F. Easmon, a Cape Coast paper published his correspondence with the War Office about training African doctors, to show that thirty years earlier there had been prejudice against them.[5] But when J. Mensah Sarbah published his *Fanti National Constitution* in 1906 he did not mention Horton's influence on the members of the Fanti Confederation.[6] Nor does his name appear in Casely Hayford's published works. When Magnus Sampson brought out an edition of Hayford's speeches in 1951, with an introduction containing a rollcall of West African national leaders, Blyden

---

4. *Watchman,* Oct. 31, 1883.
5. David Kimble, *A Political History of Ghana* (London, 1963), p. 67n.
6. This deficiency was made up for by Dr. Hollis Lynch in his introduction to the second edition, published in 1968.

and Brew were included, Horton was omitted. George Padmore left him out of *The Gold Coast Revolution*, published in 1953, and only mentioned him in passing, as a distinguished Creole of the past, in his *Pan-Africanism or Communism* in 1956.

Nor was Horton commemorated across the Atlantic. W. H. Ferris did not include him among the "Forty Colored Immortals" in his two-volume *The African Abroad* published in 1913. Only one of his books, *Letters on the Political Condition of the Gold Coast,* appeared in Monroe N. Work's standard *A Bibliography of the Negro* of 1928.

Not until 1963, with the publication of David Kimble's *A Political History of Ghana,* was his important contribution to West African nationalism belatedly recognized. In the following year the late Lloyd Gwam published an article on his social and political ideas.[7] It was left to a German scholar, Imanuel Geiss, to call attention to him as a pioneer of the policies of educational and economic development which were being followed in West Africa in the 1950's and 1960's.[8] Gradually his works were reprinted. *West African Countries and Peoples* appeared in 1968, edited by George Shepperson, *Letters on the Political Condition of the Gold Coast* in 1970, edited by E. A. Ayandele, and in 1969 Davidson Nicol brought out a comprehensive selection from his writings with illuminating annotations.

It is no wonder that Horton attracted attention in the early 1960's, the bright confident morning of African independence. In that honeymoon era of euphoric optimism, when Africans and Europeans laid aside old animosities, and a golden future seemed to await the newly independent African states, his visions appeared to have come true. Colonial rule was vanishing. Everywhere African governments were investing massively in the policies he had advocated—economic development, education, medical and sanitary reform. Horton could be unhesitatingly acclaimed as the prophet of the new Africa.

Now, in the 1970's, his optimism seems perhaps less well grounded. The clouds have gathered again over Africa. White

---

7. L. C. Gwam, "The Social and Political Ideas of Dr James Africanus Beale Horton," *Ibadan,* xix (1964), pp. 10-18.
8. Imanuel Geiss, *Panafrikanismus* (Frankfurt, 1968), pp. 62, 96, 320, 327-28.

racism, muted in the early 1960's, is on the offensive once more. The ostensibly independent African states seem dangerously dependent on foreign initiatives. The massive economic development often turns out to be chiefly for the benefit of foreigners. Neo-colonialism succeeds colonialism. Even education raises as many complex problems as it solves. Optimism smells like dishonesty, and Horton with his optimistic faith in African progress seems almost a suspect guide.

Yet to abandon his faith is to abandon the future. "Where there is no vision the people perish." Horton's people on both sides of the Atlantic still need his vision.

SELECTED BIBLIOGRAPHY

MANUSCRIPT SOURCES

Horton Manuscripts
If Horton's private papers survive I have not been able to trace them.
The great-grandson of his London agent, Sir Charles McGrigor, has no
records of his business activities. Nor have papers come to light in
Freetown.

There is, however, a small Horton collection (CAI/0117) in the
archives of the Church Missionary Society in London. Many of his
letters and reports survive in the Colonial Office records in the Public
Record Office, London, in the series C.O. 96 (Gold Coast) and C.O. 267
(Sierra Leone). There are documents written by him in the Royal Army
Medical Museum, Aldershot, Hampshire, and one letter among the
Blackwood Manuscripts in the National Library of Scotland, Edinburgh.
His manuscript M.D. thesis is in the library of the University of Edin-
burgh.

Manuscript Sources for Horton's Life
Much of Horton's early life can be traced from records in the Church
Missionary Society's archives. The details of his official career are scattered through the Colonial Office records in the Public Record Office,
in the series C.O. 87 (Gambia), C.O. 96 (Gold Coast), C.O. 267 (Sierra
Leone), and in the Colonial Office Confidential Prints, series formerly
C.O. 806, now reclassified as C.O. 879. There are a few references to him
in the War Office records in the Public Record Office, but many of the
routine papers which would have provided details of his army life have
been destroyed.

Details of his academic career are available in the manuscript collections of King's College, London, and the University of Edinburgh. There are a few references to him in documents in the Sierra Leone National Archives, and in the cape coast legal records preserved in the Ghana National Archives. The Registrar-General's Office in Freetown has records of his purchases and sales of Freetown property and a copy of his will; another copy is in Somerset House, London.

PRINTED SOURCES

Horton's Printed Works
Horton published the following books:
The Medical Topography of the West Coast of Africa (London, 1859).
Geological Constitution of Ahanta, Gold Coast (Freetown, 1862).
Political Economy of British Western Africa (London, 1865).
Physical and Medical Climate and Meteorology of the West Coast of Africa (London, 1867).
West African Countries and Peoples (London, 1868).
Guinea Worm, or Dracunculus (London, 1868).
Letters on the Political Condition of the Gold Coast (London, 1870).
The Diseases of Tropical Climates and their Treatment (London, 1874).
The Diseases of Tropical Climates and their Treatment (2nd Ed. Revised: London, 1879).

Two have been reprinted: *West African Countries and Peoples,* edited by George Shepperson (Edinburgh, 1969), and *Letters on the Political Condition of the Gold Coast,* edited by E. A. Ayandele (London, 1970). A selection from his writings has been published under the title *Africanus Horton: The Dawn of Nationalism in Modern Africa* (London, 1969), with introduction and commentaries by Davidson Nicol.

Horton published two articles, "Analysis of the Red Earth or Soil of Sierra Leone," in the Army Medical Department Annual Report for 1866 *(Parliamentary Papers,* 1867-68, XLIV, 333-34), and "Guinea Worm amongst a detachment of the 2nd West India Regiment on the West Coast of Africa," in the Army Medical Department Annual Report for 1868 *(Parliamentary Papers,* 1870, XLIII, 335-36).

He wrote letters under his own name to the *African Times,* published in London, of 23 May 1864, 23 January 1865, and 23 April 1866, and other contributions which appeared there anonymously. A letter he wrote to *The Negro,* a Freetown newspaper, was reprinted in T. J. Thompson, *The Jubilee and Centenary Volume of Fourah Bay College, Sierra Leone* (Freetown, 1930), which also contained extracts from his will. A speech he made in London in 1882 was reported in *Journal of the Royal Society of Arts,* 30 (1881-82), 782-83.

Printed Sources for Horton's Life
Details of his university career can be found in the *Edinburgh University Calendars,* 1858-60. Details of his army career are in W. Johnston,

Roll of Army Medical Service (London, 1917), and in the annual *Army Lists.* A. A. Gore, *The Story of our Services under the Crown—A Historical Sketch of the Army Medical Staff* (London, 1879) supplies information about the medical services of the British army in West Africa.

The *African Times* contains many references to him; so do the contemporary Freetown newspapers *Independent, West African Reporter, Watchman,* and *Freetown Express,* the Cape Coast *Gold Coast Times,* and the Lagos *Eagle and Lagos Critic* and *Lagos Observer.* There are also references to him and his family in Freetown newspapers published after his death, particularly the *Sierra Leone Weekly News, Sierra Leone Times,* and *The Colony and Provincial Reporter.*

Information relating to him or his interests can be found in the following Parliamentary Papers—P.P. 1865 V, *Report of the Select Committee of the House of Commons;* P.P. 1865 XXXIII, 329-35, *Report on the Ashantee Expedition;* P.P. 1889 LIV, 175-87, *Report on the Gold Coast Mines.*

He is mentioned in R. F. Burton and V. L. Cameron, *To the Gold Coast for Gold* (London, 1883). R. F. Burton, *Wanderings in West Africa* (London, 1863), and Edward W. Blyden, *Christianity, Islam and the Negro Race* (London, 1887) are indirectly relevant to the study of his life.

His ideas are discussed in Imanuel Geiss, *Panafrikanismus* (Frankfurt, 1968), Robert W. July, *The Origins of Modern African Thought* (London, 1968), L. C. Gwam, "The Social and Political Ideas of Dr James Africanus Beale Horton," *Ibadan,* 19 (1964), and George Shepperson, "An early African Graduate," *University of Edinburgh Gazette,* 32 (1962).

For the background to his life in Sierra Leone, see John Peterson, *Province of Freedom* (London, 1969); Arthur T. Porter, *Creoledom* (London, 1963); Christopher Fyfe, *A History of Sierra Leone* (London, 1962), and *Sierra Leone Inheritance* (London, 1964). For the Gold Coast background, see David Kimble, *A Political History of Ghana, 1850–1928* (Oxford, 1963); Douglas Coombs, *The Gold Coast, Britain and the Netherlands, 1850-1874* (London, 1963); and Francis Agbodeka, "The Fanti Confederacy, 1865-69," *Transactions of the Historical Society of Ghana,* 7 (1964), 82-123. For the Gambia background see J. M. Gray, *A History of the Gambia* (Cambridge, 1940).

Two unpublished theses contribute valuable background information: Lamin Abdou Mbye, "Senior African Civil Servants in British West Africa, 1808-1895" (University of Birmingham, Ph.D. thesis, 1969), and Edward Dixon, "The American Negro in Scotland in the Nineteenth Century" (University of Edinburgh, M.Litt. thesis, 1970).

For the historical evolution of the theories of race discussed in Chapter IV, see Philip D. Curtin, *The Image of Africa* (Madison, 1964).

Other important background books include:

J. F. Ade Ajayi, *Christian Missions in Nigeria, 1841-1891* (London, 1965).

E. A. Ayandele, *Holy Johnson* (London, 1970).

Kwamina B. Dickson, *A Historical Geography of Ghana* (Cambridge, 1969).

J. D. Hargreaves, *Prelude to the Partition of West Africa* (London, 1963).

Hollis R. Lynch, *Edward Wilmot Blyden: Pan-Negro Patriot, 1832-1912* (London, 1967).

Henry S. Wilson, ed., *Origins of West African Nationalism* (London, 1969).

INDEX